*To The Spirit of God
alive in the heart of man -*

Sri Akhenaton

TABLE OF CONTENTS

PREFACE

By definition, Meditation is the process by which the conscious mind is freed of all thoughts, thereby allowing the Peace, Harmony, Wisdom and Love of the Universe to immerse mortal consciousness in the benevolent sea of Divine Truth. In this text, however, we approach Meditation from a slightly different perspective. In this instance, Meditation is defined as the infusion of the conscious mind with The Divine Light Vibrations of The One Infinite Creator to facilitate the conscious attunement to The Divine Precepts of Universal Law - Patience, Compassion, Wisdom, Mercy, Serenity and Love in The Light of One. It is this attunement process we define that initiates the unfoldment of the "God-self" state of consciousness, which allows mortal man to access and consciously exist within The Infinite Body of God.

LoveLight Meditations are based in ancient teachings from Lemuria, Atlantis, Pre-Dynastic Egypt and India, and are designed to assist each soul incarnate being in utilizing The Divine Light Vibrations amplified through the Quartz/Mineral Kingdom to enhance the quality of Earthly life. It is through the conscious attunement to and the applications of Divine Light Vibrations that mankind comes to learn about man's inherent Light-minded nature, and the truth about man's innate, Divine abilities as children of God.

The procedures outlined in this text were developed over many, many years through an initiate understanding of the dynamics of Divine Energy Transmissions, and through the acceptance of the nature and function of Spiritual Practices from Ancient Traditions. The Meditations that follow are described in a manner designed to assist the contemporary Spiritual Aspirant in the Unfoldment Process that affects The Greater Good of All Creation, and ultimately leads the seeker of Truth toward the assimilation of The Lessons of Existence. Each Meditation is structured specifically to impact upon mortal consciousness to encourage development from the stage of soul incarnate to the state of evolved being - one who understands and unilaterally applies The Divine Wisdom of One throughout the realm of galactic existence.

After practicing LoveLight Meditations for a short time, you will observe that your thought process is enhanced by a deeper sense of connection to all living things upon Planet Earth, and by your growing awareness of your personal connection to The Infinite Body of God. It is the evolution of the absolute understanding that The Consciousness of God lives in your own intuitive soul that is the single, most significant factor that allows acceptance and facilitates implementation of The Wisdom of One. It is therefore our prayer that all who contemplate this text will discover the Meditations that follow to be useful and comforting in the journey of Soul Evolution, and that each reader will learn to heed the guidance of the intuitive voice that speaks with The Conviction and Grace of Universal Conscience.

Shalom, Adonai, Shalom

Sri Akhenaton

8

CRYSTAL
COMMUNION

INTRODUCTION

LoveLight Meditation is a "Trans-Cultural", synergetic approach to Spirituality that is based in practices from ancient Spiritual Traditions. In its contemporary form, LoveLight Meditation techniques combine recognizable elements and practices from Native American Shamanism, Christian Mysticism, Hindu and Yogic Traditions, Tibetan Buddhism and West African Spiritualism to stimulate the awakening of Divine Consciousness. Utilizing Prayers, Invocations, Visualizations, Mantras, Affirmations and Quartz Crystals and Minerals to infuse mortal consciousness with The Divine Light Vibrations of The One Infinite Creator, LoveLight Meditation is designed to assist the evolutionary process by which mankind learns to access the God-self state of consciousness. It is through accessing and accepting the God-self that man consciously becomes an active, component part of The Infinite Body of God, with the self-serving aspects of ego-consciousness and linear thought finding transformation in The Light of One. It is the acceptance of the God-self that allows man to become a willing instrument for the transmission of Divine Love.

LoveLight Meditation stimulates the active process of Soul Evolution, which in turn stimulates man's ability to access the memory systems of the soul that facilitate the development of the "intuitive voice", the inner sense of "Knowingness" that transcends the limits of linear thought. Additionally, by

11

infusing The Divine Light Vibrations amplified through Quartz Crystals and Minerals into the physical and auric bodies, mankind learns to access The Knowledge of Creation through intuitive guidance, thus discovering how to conscionably implement practical aspects of Universal Law upon the Earth Plane. It is then that mortal man will have evolved to the level of consciousness that facilitates the release of discordant energy/behavior patterns that have impeded the development of God-Realized Consciousness.

It is the alignment of man's energy systems to Universal Light Vibrations that is the awakening to The Consciousness of One. It is man's conscious choice to awaken dormant understanding and Wisdom that ultimately leads to the comprehension of Divine Will. It is the acceptance of mankind's role in Divine Order that allows man to commune with all things born of Creation. It is mankind's responsibility to evolve in mind, body and spirit, thereby exemplifying the Light-minded nature that is The Conscience of God alive in mortal form.

LoveLight Meditation's simple system of Meditation techniques gently guides the seeker of enlightened consciousness into the inner sanctuaries of evolved being. With emphasis placed upon that which is "good and right" for the individual, that is, acknowledging individual readiness to assimilate spiraling levels of Higher Consciousness, LoveLight Meditation techniques offer each soul incarnate the opportunity to visualize his or her life-condition in terms of Universal Law dynamics. This affords each individual the choice of sustaining and enhancing productive behaviors and/or breaking karmic patterns that inhibit Serenity, Patience, Compassion, Mercy, Wisdom and Love - the Light-minded behavior that is The Oneness of Creation.

LoveLight Meditation ushers in states of serene clarity that facilitate conscious well-being and assist in transmuting problematic life-conditions by infusing the individual with Divine Light Vibrations of The Infinite One - The Supreme Source of Light, Life, Wisdom and Love that is The Evolved Consciousness of the Universe. In addition, LoveLight Meditation stimulates and grounds the understanding that all things, from unicellular creatures and minerals to towering redwoods and mammals, all Kingdoms upon Mother Earth are sacred in Divine Order. Mankind's understanding and appreciation for all forms of life finds greater expression when man is in attunement with Universal Light/Life Vibrations. With diligence and patience, the Meditations that follow can aid the earnest seeker of enlightenment in uncovering and nurturing his/her innate Light-minded nature, and assist in transforming mortal existence into an ever-expanding experience of Divine Love.

I

LoveLight Meditations

MEDITATION GUIDELINES
Invocations, Prayers and Affirmations

1.

To prepare for your Meditation, select a room that is quiet and softly illuminated. Preferably, the room you choose will be the same room you use for each of your Meditation periods. Try to schedule your Meditations for approximately the same time and duration on the days that you choose to Meditate. Initially, thirty to ninety minutes is an adequate length of time for Meditation, and daily Meditation is the preferred practice.

Choose a seated position that is comfortable for you. *(Whether you choose to employ a traditional floor position or are more comfortable seated in a straight-backed chair with both feet flat on the floor and hands resting on the knees or thighs, the result of your Meditation will not be significantly different.)* Clothing that is worn during Meditation should fit loosely about the body, and shoes should not be worn. *(See Illustrations 1 and 2)*

Now, select a Clear Quartz Crystal *(a single or double terminated Generator is suggested)* about palm-size or larger that will serve as your Meditation Partner. Cleanse and bless your Crystal in advance by washing it in cool, running water, then place the Crystal in direct sunlight for an afternoon. While you

ILLUSTRATION 1

TRADITIONAL MEDITATION POSTURE

ILLUSTRATION 2

MEDITATION POSTURE SEATED IN A CHAIR

wash the Crystal, consciously transmit your desire that the Crystal release all discordant energy it may have stored in its matrix. All Crystals and Minerals used in Meditation and in Healing Facilitation should first be cleansed and blessed in this manner.

Once in a comfortable position, begin a rhythmic breathing sequence by inhaling deeply though the nose, holding the breath for three seconds and slowly exhaling from the mouth. As you inhale, visualize cleansing Golden/White Light Vibrations entering your body through your nose, traveling down your trachea, filling your lungs, chest cavity and heart center with warm, glowing LoveLight Sensations. As you exhale, visualize discordant vibrations, tension, confusion and stress leaving your body through your mouth in dark, cloudy swirls of energy. Bless yourself and your discordant vibrations in The Name of Yahweh, by The Spirit of Christ Jesus, as you cast these dissonant vibrations unto the ether to find Peaceful resolution.

Now, pick up your Clear Quartz Crystal with your left hand and begin to gaze upon it, observing the unique features it has to offer *(rainbows, Chlorite phantoms, healed fractures, mists, etc.)*. Allow your consciousness to merge with your Crystal. Gently stroke the Crystal with the index finger of your right hand and silently repeat the words, *"Attune, Balance, Integrate, Ground."* Close your eyes and repeat these words several times. Soon you may experience warm, tingling sensations in your hands and fingers. Your Crystal will seem to come alive in your hand, radiating a warm sensation that was not present earlier. *(See Illustration 3)*

ILLUSTRATION 3

CRYSTAL GAZING & ATTUNEMENT

2.

The Meditation sequence has begun. Now, offer a silent Prayer for Blessing and for The Invocation of The Light of God. The Prayer that we have found to be most effective is as follows:

LOVELIGHT PRAYER/INVOCATION

Almighty Yah*, Great Spirit of Light,

By The Spirit of Christ Jesus**, in Thee do I trust.

Protect me, Father; Guide me, Father; Strengthen me, Father;

Cleanse me, Father; Heal me, Father.

Fill me with The Light of Thy Presence, Father.

Surround me, Father, with Archangel Michael in the East,

Archangel Gabriel in the West, Archangel Raphael in the North,

Archangel Uriel in the South, and grant me communion, Father,

With Thy Legion of Light.

Almighty Yah, Great Spirit of Light,

By The Spirit of Christ Jesus, in Thee do I trust.

---

* *Yah is an abbreviation for the name Yahweh, The Creator of modern man.*

** *The names Buddha, Krishna, Mohammed, Enoch & Melchizedek may be included with the name Christ Jesus, as These are all Divine Vibrations of The Yahweh Entity.*

The rhythmic breathing that was begun prior to this Prayer is to be continued throughout the recitation of the Prayer. You will notice that your breathing will become more and more shallow.

3.

Following The Prayer for Blessing/Invocation, recite The 23rd Psalm, while continuing your rhythmic breathing:

THE 23RD PSALM

The Lord is my shepherd; I shall not want.

He maketh me to lie down in green pastures:

He leadeth me beside the still waters.

He restoreth my soul:

He leadeth me in the paths of righteousness for His name's sake.

Yea, though I walk through the valley of the shadow of death,

I will fear no evil:

for Thou art with me;

Thy rod and Thy staff they comfort me.

Thou preparest a table before me in the presence of mine enemies:

Thou anointest my head with oil;

my cup runneth over.

Surely goodness and mercy shall follow me all the days of my life:

and I will dwell in the house of The Lord forever.

4.

Affirmations are now verbalized to instill in the conscious mind the precepts of Universal Truth, and to merge the conscious mind with the subconscious motivations for Peace and Harmony. The following Affirmations are ones that we have found will produce the desired results and are to be repeated slowly as a set three times:

AFFIRMATIONS

I am Patience

I am Compassion

I am Wisdom

I am Mercy

I am Serenity

I am Love

I am Selfless in The Light of One

Continue rhythmic breathing throughout your Affirmations.

If Tingshaw *(Tibetan Meditation Cymbals)* are used in conjunction with the Affirmations, the Tingshaw are to be struck once prior to each Affirmation.

Upon completing the Affirmations, continue your rhythmic breathing. You will notice that a state of Tranquility has been reached. Allow your conscious mind to be further stilled by concentrating on your rhythmic breathing that has now become very shallow.

You have now ascended into the realm of LoveLight Meditation. Savor the stillness and sense of Peace that fill you. Feel your mind and body freed of confusion, discordant emotions, tension and stress. Feel the burden of daily responsibilities lifted from your shoulders, as sensations of weightlessness encompass you. Hear the sound of your heart beating in Harmony with the Universe. Listen as the conscience of your intuitive soul fills you with the understanding of The Oneness of all Creation. Watch as The Light of God permeates every fiber of your being with the radiance of Love. And know that now you have accessed and activated The Divine Light Vibration within you that connects your consciousness to The Infinite Body of God.

5.

When you are ready to return to the reality of your Meditation room, simply count backwards from ten to one. At the count of one, open your eyes and breathe deeply several times. Remain seated. Allow yourself the time required to reintegrate into third dimension reality. Savor the LoveLight Vibrations that fill you as you reflect upon your Meditation experience.

It should be stated here that individual perceptions and depth of Meditations vary, and are dependent upon desire, conviction, patience, motivation and readiness to accept and utilize the principles set forth herein. Even though every person is capable of learning to Meditate, individual experiences and levels of Spiritual Attunement may be quite diverse, and as such one may become engaged in comparing personal Meditation experiences to the Meditation experiences of others. Subsequently, comparisons and judgements made about the relative stage of enlightenment and the assignment of levels of accomplishment or lack thereof to the experience of Meditation serves only to facilitate the maintenance of illusions generated by egocentric drives. It is our position that such comparisons are both unnecessary and counterproductive, as indeed the state or level of evolution identified as one's personal reality is precisely the stage of consciousness one requires to facilitate moments of individual Karmic Resolution and the continued, conscious evolution of the soul. What this means is that personal experiences of Meditation are indeed "good and right" for the individual as experienced, no matter what the depth or the nature of the experience might be, as in truth there will be personal thought and behavior patterns revealed through the practice and experience of Meditation that ultimately will facilitate learning The Lessons of Existence.

Try to allow your intuitive wisdom to guide you in the understanding of Meditation sequences (whether your Meditations are rich in visual references or whether you only experience minor physical sensations), and in accepting the state and purpose of any given stage of evolution. Allow yourself to accept the references and sensations transmitted by your intuitive wisdom, as therein lies The Wisdom and The Truth that is The Consciousness of The Living God Spirit.

SUPPLEMENTAL NOTES
ON MEDITATION

BREATHING

Rhythmic Breathing is essential in the practice of Meditation. Drawing the breath in deeply through the nose and slowly exhaling from the mouth serves to relax the body, and centers the attention on the Meditation ahead. During the course of your Meditation, as you relax more and more, your breathing will become progressively more shallow, and the sound of your heartbeat will become wonderfully resonant. *(Additionally, focusing a fixed gaze upward through your third eye chakra can facilitate a more expedient transition into states of elevated consciousness.)* After a time, you may choose to both inhale and exhale through your nose, but initially it is recommended that you inhale through your nose and exhale from your mouth.

The most efficient manner of executing rhythmic breathing exercises is individually determined by breathing in cadence with one's heartbeat. With the index and second fingers of your right hand, take your pulse at the left wrist. Feel the cadence and begin to count in rhythm with your pulse, *one-two, one-two, one-two.* Quiet your mind and focus upon the cadence of your pulse, *one-two, one-two, one-two.* Feel the cadence. *(The cadence of your pulse may fluctuate depending upon the time of day and physical or emotional factors in operation at the time your pulse is taken. It is recommended that you take your pulse at different times of the day to establish your true cadence.)* Now, begin to count in rhythm with your pulse, *one-two-three-four-five-six, one-two-three-four-five-six.* Repeat this sequence again and again, *one-two-three-four-five-six, one-two-three-four-five-six.* This will be your cadence for inhaling, holding your breath and exhaling. Relax and continue to count in rhythm with the cadence of your pulse until you feel comfortable with the pattern.

Now, begin your rhythmic breathing by closing your eyes and silently repeating the words, *"Attune, Balance, Integrate, Ground"*, several times to assist in focusing, balancing and grounding your energies. Next, silently repeat the words, *"Almighty Yah, Great Spirit of Light, by The Spirit of Christ Jesus, in Thee do I trust."* Relax. Inhale deeply through the nose to the count of *one-two-three-four-five-six*, hold your breath to the count of *one-two-three* and exhale from your mouth to the count of *one-two-three-four-five-six*. Repeat this sequence a minimum of seven times per sitting and you will soon notice a much deeper sense of Peace and Tranquility as a result of this exercise. You will also notice that your Meditations will become more profound and that you will develop a comforting, enduring sense of inner knowingness.

One of the visualization techniques that we have found to be most effective in association with rhythmic breathing is the procedure for bonding with the Akasha, which is the etheric, elemental material from which all physical reality or matter is created. In effect, the Akasha is the building material or sub-atomic matter from which the tangible, physical Universe is formed. It has been said that the entirety of Universal Creation was simply a "materialized thought form" offered by The Supreme, Universal God-Head, that which we identify as The Infinite One. To bond with the Akasha allows mortal man to begin the process of consciously and intuitively comprehending the very essence of Universal Conscience by participating in the flow of the energy of Creation.

To visualize the Akasha, simply close your eyes and allow

yourself to visualize billions upon billions of sub-microscopic pin-points of Golden/White Light energy twinkling all around you. Close your eyes for a second and try to visualize and feel the Golden/White pinpoints of Divine Light Energy that form the network of the Akasha. (*See Illustration 4*)

Begin your rhythmic breathing sequence by focusing, balancing and grounding as was described earlier. Take your pulse again to reestablish your correct breathing cadence and begin by inhaling through the nose, holding the breath and exhaling from the mouth. Now, visualize the Akasha surrounding you. See the billions upon billions of pinpoints of Golden/White Light Energy around you. As you inhale, visualize the Akasha entering your nose, traveling down your trachea and filling your lungs and heart center with radiant, Golden/White Light Energy of Life. As you exhale, visualize the Akasha leaving your body in Golden/White Light Energy that you release from your mouth. Visualize the Golden/White Light network of Akasha surrounding you as you continue your rhythmic breathing sequence and feel every cell of your body from head to toe begin to open to absorb the Divine Golden/White Light of the Akasha. Feel yourself begin to resonate with the elemental source of Creation. Feel yourself surrounded by and infused with the very essence of Life and The Consciousness of Divine Truth. Allow yourself to be as One with The God Spirit alive in all things born of Creation.

NOTE: As with all exercises, visualizations and Meditations, it is recommended that focus, balance and grounding be initiated by silently repeating the words, *"Attune, Balance, Integrate, Ground"*, at least three times. Then it is recommended that the following statement be silently repeated, *"Almighty Yah, Great Spirit of Light, by The Spirit of Christ Jesus, in Thee do I trust."* This statement proclaims Universal Allegiance to the

ILLUSTRATION 4

VISUALIZATION OF THE AKASHA

conscionable application of The Wisdom of One as promulgated by The Council of Twelve.

MUSIC AND SOUND

The purpose of the Meditation Guidelines is to provide a systematic procedure for achieving inner Peace and to assist in the unfoldment of the God-self state of being. These techniques are designed to usher in Tranquility and Universal Light Vibrations by stilling the conscious mind and allowing the wisdom of the intuitive self to surface and guide human behavior. It is the contemplation of silence and the understanding that Peace and Spiritual Attunement are produced as the result of accessing inner wisdom that are the focus of the aforementioned Meditation Guidelines.

There are, however, notable exceptions to the strict adherence to the contemplation of silence. One exception to this statement is the use of Tibetan Cymbals, Tingshaw, and singing bowls *(both Quartz Crystal and Tibetan Brass types)* during the verbalization of Affirmations. The pure, rich tones of these spiritual tools ring with The Vibration of Oneness, and upon being sounded, immediately clear the environment of disruptive, discordant vibrations. Since the purpose of Affirmations is to instill in the conscious mind those constructs that foster "The Way of The One", the use of Tingshaw and singing bowls is certainly encouraged. The sounds produced by these instruments do not distract or lead one away from the purpose of Meditation; rather, the Tingshaw and singing bowls escort the user toward a deeper understanding of and an appreciation for The Absolute Beauty of Oneness.

Another exception to the practice of observing silence during Meditation is the use of audible Mantras or chants that invoke Divine Light Vibrations. *(Mantras can be and are frequently practiced silently, which allows one who is experienced in the use of Mantras to generate an even higher vibratory rate than that achieved with audible chants.)* By verbalizing sacred words and syllables, one can raise resonance patterns and enter altered states of consciousness. It is during states of altered consciousness that man communes with The Conscience of The Universal One and learns to access his/her personal connection to The Infinite Body of God. Many cultures and Spiritual Traditions worldwide practice the use of Mantras or chants to gain access to higher spiritual realms, which facilitates the ability to perform unusual feats of tolerance to pain and physical endurance that defy logical explanation.

Om (pronounced Aum) is a Mantra that is said to be The Universal Sound of Creation. Used in Hindu and Buddhist Traditions, Om is chanted to center, focus and to connect one's consciousness to The Universal Energy of Creation. Other Mantras such as *Om Mani Padme Hum ("Oh, Jewel of The Lotus, Amen")*, *Om Tat Sat Om ("O Thou Self Existent One")* and *Om Namo Bhagavate Vasudevaya (a salutation to "The Universal God-Head")* are chanted daily in Meditation and Prayer in India, Tibet, China and many other parts of the Middle East (and the world). It has been our experience that Mantras can be most effective when practiced in conjunction with rhythmic breathing exercises. After practicing Mantras for a short time, the profound spiritual impact that these Divine Vibrations have upon the evolving consciousness of mortal man becomes self-evident. Only after feeling the resonance and the sense of Divine Peace that the word *"Om"* can produce in Meditation can one truly know the value of such sacred words and timeless practice.

Cassette tapes designed for relaxation, those with enchanting sounds of nature, or simply tapes with melodious orchestral arrangements, can in some cases prove distracting. Though relaxation tapes and music can be very helpful in tension and stress reduction, it is suggested that music of any kind not be played during your Meditation sequences, at least until you are familiar with the basic techniques.

AFFIRMATIONS

As has been discussed earlier, Affirmations are used to assist in the merging of the conscious mind with subconscious motivations for Peace and Harmony. The subconscious motivations addressed here form the body of intuitive wisdom housed by the soul essence. It is the memory system of the soul that is The Light Vibration of Divine Conscience that seeks integration with and expression through the physical self. This process utilizes the reinforcements provided by Affirmations in facilitating the desired results. By consciously affirming statements of Patience, Compassion, Wisdom, Mercy, Serenity and Selfless Love in The Light of One, which are the core motivations for Light-minded behavior, the etheric self finds viable expression upon Mother Earth and Spiritual Attunement is achieved.

Affirmations that are used in LoveLight Meditations can be used at any time to generate balance, focus and grounding, thereby facilitating the development and expression of the God-self state of consciousness. It should be noted however, that for the most efficient assimilation of the vibrations of the Affirmations, one should examine the deepest meaning of the concepts the Affirmations promote. It is suggested that one ask the questions: *"What is Patience, and why is Patience desirable? What is Compassion, and why is Compassion desirable? What is Wisdom, ...?"* and so on. Examine the Affirmations, their implications and applications to yourself, then to your family, your friends, the global population, the other Kingdoms of the Planet and finally to Mother Earth. When the dynamics of the Affirmations are fully accepted and implemented, then the highest degree of LoveLight Vibration can be realized in the physical plane.

Other Affirmations that can be used in conjunction with or apart from LoveLight Meditations are:

✳

I am Love

I have Love for all Creation

I am Compassion

I have Compassion for all Creation

I am Mercy

I have Mercy for all Creation

I am Light

I see The Light of God in all Creation

✳

*

I am Patience

I have Patience for all Creation

I am Patience

I have Patience for the impatient

I am Patience

I have Patience for myself

I am Patience

I have Patience for all Creation

*

I am Serenity

I offer Serenity to all Creation

I am Love

I offer Love to all Creation

I am Mercy

I offer Mercy to all Creation

I am Light

I offer The Light of God to all Creation

*

SYMBOLS AND STATES
OF EXPANDED CONSCIOUSNESS

The use of symbols and geometric shapes to achieve states of expanded consciousness began with modern man's first attempts to achieve conscious union with the pervasive, omnipresent vibration of The Living God Spirit. Through Meditation upon specific patterns and sequences of shapes and symbols, mortal consciousness can be freed from the "cosmic illusion" of Maya, the principle of compelling duality, to achieve the state of Grace that is the realization of The Oneness of Creation. By allowing the barriers that impede the journey of Soul Evolution to be dissolved, that is, choosing to transmute the drives of the ego-self, mortal man can then achieve the ultimate experience of enlightenment, transcending Maya and bonding with The Spirit of The Infinite One. Five symbols and shapes that we use to achieve states of expanded consciousness are shown in *Chart I.*

Diagram 1 shows a progression of six shapes and symbols. It is revealed that each symbol pattern incorporates and builds upon the elements of the preceding pattern. Each symbol pattern is to be gazed upon for one to three minutes *(Figures 1 through 6).* At the end of the gazing period *(try to hold your gaze without blinking),* close your eyes and visualize the symbol pattern you have just seen. Allow yourself time to fully engage each symbol pattern in relaxed visualization before proceeding to the next pattern. If you become drowsy or feel yourself being drawn into the center of the symbol pattern, simply flow with the process and close your eyes to begin visualizing the symbol pattern that you have just seen.

CHART I

SYMBOLS & SHAPES USED TO STIMULATE STATES OF EXPANDED CONSCIOUSNESS

TRIANGLE
Symbolizes unity of mind/body/spirit complex

CIRCLE
Symbolizes completion, resolution, unity

SIX-POINTED STAR
Symbolizes elements of Divine Truth; symbolizes the union of mortal consciousness with the evolved soul

FIVE-POINTED STAR
Symbolizes the elements of earth, air, fire, water and the ability of the conscious mind to direct the activities of these elemental forces; symbolizes the doorway to Universal expansion of consciousness

ANKH
The Key of Life that symbolizes the immortality of the soul

DIAGRAM 1

One

Two

Three

Four

Five

Six

To prepare for your Meditation, begin by focusing, balancing and grounding as outlined earlier, offer your Statement of Allegiance and initiate a rhythmic breathing sequence. Now, gaze upon the first symbol *(Figure 1)* for one to three minutes. Close your eyes and visualize the first symbol you have seen taking form in the center of your third eye chakra. Hold this visualization for one to three minutes. *(Visualization of symbols and patterns can be held for longer periods than three minutes, but it is recommended that the minimum length of time for visualization not be less than one minute.)* Open your eyes and begin to gaze upon the second symbol pattern *(Figure 2)* for one to three minutes. Close your eyes and visualize the pattern you have just seen. Continue this procedure until you reach the sixth and final symbol pattern *(Figure 6)*. After gazing upon the sixth symbol pattern, close your eyes and watch as the symbol materializes at your third eye chakra. Orient the symbol pattern in such a way as to place the five-pointed star in the exact center of your third eye chakra. Allow yourself to be transported by the five-pointed star through the consciousness state of mind over matter. Allow yourself to experience the reality of expanded consciousness. Allow yourself to feel the freedom, the wonderment and Grace that await the evolved consciousness of each mortal being. Allow yourself to experience the revelation that is The Oneness of Creation.

Diagram 2 shows a second series of six symbol patterns, each of which is associated with a particular Affirmation. Each Affirmation is an element of Universal Conscience that is designed to assist mortal man in the comprehension, application and execution of Light-minded behavior. By assigning the Affirmations of Patience, Compassion, Wisdom, Mercy, Serenity and Love to each symbol combination in the progression of patterns, we are able to both awaken and instill these Divine Precepts in the conscious thoughts and behaviors of mortal life.

Prepare for your Meditation by focusing, balancing and grounding your energies as described previously. Then offer your Statement of Allegiance and begin your sequence of rhythmic breathing. Now, gaze upon the first symbol *(Figure 7)* for one to three minutes. At the end of three minutes (or sooner), close your eyes and visualize the first symbol. As you visualize the first symbol, silently repeat the associated Affirmation, *"I am Patience."* Slowly repeat the Affirmation again and again for up to five minutes. Now, open your eyes and begin to gaze upon the second symbol pattern *(Figure 8)* for one to three minutes. Again, close your eyes at the end of three minutes and begin to visualize the pattern you have just seen. While you visualize the second pattern, silently repeat the associated Affirmation, *"I am Compassion."* Slowly repeat the Affirmation again and again for up to five minutes. Continue this procedure through the third, fourth, fifth and sixth symbol patterns *(Figures 9 through 12)*. After gazing upon the sixth symbol pattern, close your eyes and visualize the pattern you have just seen. Visualize the sixth symbol pattern in the center of your third eye chakra and orient this pattern in such a way as to place the five-pointed star in the exact center of your third eye chakra. Now, silently repeat the associated Affirmation, *"I am Love."* Slowly repeat this Affirmation again and again for up to five minutes. Allow yourself to bond with the spirit of this Affirmation and realize that each of the foregoing Affirmations - Patience, Compassion, Wisdom, Mercy and Serenity, form the progression of evolved consciousness that gives birth to Selfless Love. Allow yourself to feel and to accept this blessing of Absolute Truth. Allow yourself to be at Peace in The Love and The Light that is One.

Figure 1

Figure 2

Figure 3

Figure 4

Figure 5

Figure 6

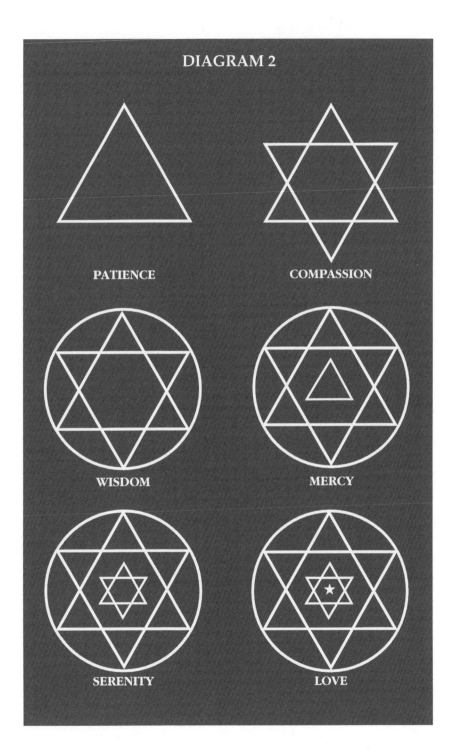

DIAGRAM 2

PATIENCE

COMPASSION

WISDOM

MERCY

SERENITY

LOVE

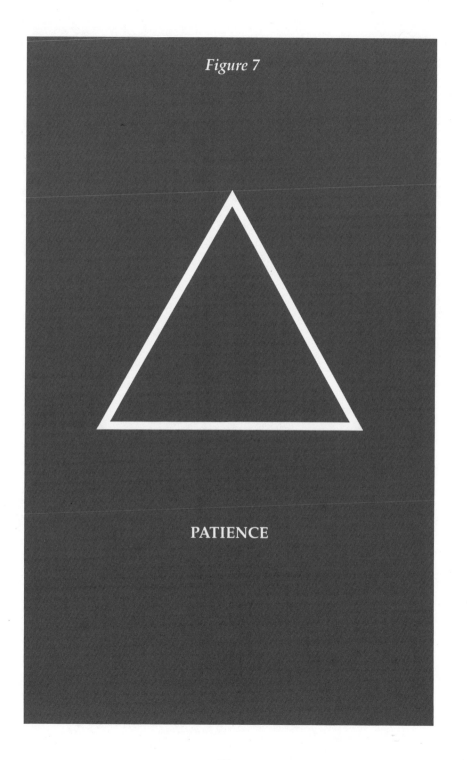

Figure 7

PATIENCE

Figure 8

COMPASSION

Figure 9

WISDOM

Figure 10

MERCY

Figure 11

SERENITY

Figure 12

LOVE

Another visualization procedure that employs symbols to achieve expanded states of consciousness we call the Golden Eagle Meditation. Golden Eagle is a majestic creature indigenous to the northern hemisphere *(about the same size as a Bald Eagle)* and is a Native American symbol that is a spirit-keeper capable of transmuting hostile, discordant energy systems that afflict mortal man. It is said that Golden Eagle is the highest flying spirit in the sky and is the only creature that can fly directly into the face of The Sun. For this reason, Golden Eagle is charged with carrying the traumatic memories, emotional wounds and energies of discordance that plague mankind into the life-giving, transformational, cleansing rays of The Sun to be Blessed and released from mortal consciousness. By allowing one's self to join with the spirit-flight of Golden Eagle, one can experience the transformation and freedom of flight that can elevate mortal consciousness to enjoy communion with The Conscience of The Universal One.

Begin your Golden Eagle Meditation by focusing, balancing and grounding your energies and offering your Statement of Allegiance. Next, close your eyes and initiate a rhythmic breathing sequence. Relax and with your eyes closed look upward through your third eye chakra. Visualize a golden triangle at your third eye chakra. *(If you have difficulty visualizing the golden triangle, simply gaze upon the triangle shown in Figure 1 for up to three minutes.)* See the golden triangle at your third eye chakra and allow your consciousness to pass through this golden portal to Galactic Truth and Transformation. Visualize a golden triangle at your third eye center and allow your consciousness to pass through this golden portal and you will find Golden Eagle awaiting you on the other side. Allow yourself to join with the spirit of Golden Eagle. Take wings and fly with Golden Eagle toward the face of The Universal Sun and watch as your fears and anxieties, tensions and stresses, emotional wounds and conflicts are Cleansed and Blessed by the Golden/White Light Rays of The Sun. Allow yourself to be freed from all discordant memories and counterproductive energies. Allow yourself to fly with Golden Eagle and experience the rites of Purification in The Light of One. Fly... Fly... Fly.... *(See Illustration 5)*

ILLUSTRATION 5

GOLDEN EAGLE VISUALIZATION

INCENSES AND ESSENTIAL OILS

Incenses and Essential Oils have been used for thousands of years in Spiritual and Religious Traditions for generating an atmosphere conducive to Meditation and Prayer, for rituals of Cleansing and Blessing, for Invocations of Divine Energies and for anointing the body. The use of smudge-sticks *(bundles of sage mixed with cedar, sweet-grass or pine resins used in Native American Ceremonies)* is recommended to clear hostile energies from your Meditation area and from your auric and physical bodies as well.

The practice of aromatherapy which is based upon ancient Ayurvedic Tradition utilizes the effects produced by various fragrances to stimulate conditions of physical, mental, emotional and spiritual well-being in mortal man. *Charts II and III* give the sensations and areas of consciousness influenced by different fragrances.

Essential Oils used to anoint and to perfume the body and Special Consecrated Oils used in bathing to cleanse the physical and auric bodies of discordant energy systems are being widely used throughout the world. The inherent quality of Essential Oils is enhanced by the Spiritual Traditions and the devotion with which Essential Oils are produced. Additionally, the Consecrated Bath Oils prepared by Spiritualists who understand the operations of Divine Light Transmission can, in addition to producing the transmutation of discordance, produce lasting sensations of Tranquility, Inner-Peace and a sense of connection to The Grace and Presence of The Living God Spirit. Allow your intuition to guide you in the selection of fragrances, for the intuitive self will always lead you toward that which is good and right for the evolution of Spiritual Conscience.

CHART II

FRAGRANCE LIST

1. Agarwood - clears hostile/discordant energy systems from environment
2. Amber - cleansing for internal organs; benevolent, calming and protecting
3. Cedar - purifying aroma that cleanses spiritual vibrations
4. Copal - resin used by Aztecs and Mayans to purify and to invoke energies in rituals and ceremonies
5. Frankincense - invokes strength of conviction while dispelling moods of depression, uncertainty and irrational behavior
6. Gardenia - sweet, uplifting, purifying aroma facilitates healing of heart chakra states
7. Gum Benzoin - resin used to cleanse and to invoke benevolent energies
8. Gum Mastic - resin used to intensify etheric consciousness
9. Henna - sweet-scented stimulant of dream states
10. Jasmine - invigorating, intoxicating aroma aids in lessening mental stress and depression
11. Juniper - cleansing, fresh-scented agent used to dispel discordant energies
12. Lavender - soothes and calms the nerves
13. Lotus - opens crown chakra and aids in awakening third eye perceptions; stimulates intuitive and conscious states of etheric presence
14. Musk - aids in developing personal will and conviction; helps to stimulate psychic energy
15. Myrrh - provides atmosphere that stimulates mental activity and heightens clarity of perception
16. Narcissus - offers transformational energy to soothe emotional energies
17. Rose - opens the heart chakra with sweet, purifying aroma
18. Sage - removes discordant vibrations from the environment
19. Sandalwood - provides calming vibrations and aromas conducive to Meditation and Spiritual Invocation
20. Sweet Grass - provides cleansing energy that invokes benevolent vibrations
21. Tuberose - sweet, benevolent scent that facilitates healing of heart chakra energies
22. Violet - softens charged emotions of aggression, hostility and discontent
23. Ylang-Ylang - calms emotions of anger and disappointment

CHART III

FRAGRANCE CHART

1. *Facilitates Healing and Opening of Heart Chakra:*
   - Gardenia
   - Lavender
   - Rose
   - Tuberose

2. *Calms, Soothes and Strengthens Mental and Emotional States:*
   - Amber *(internal organs)*
   - Myrrh
   - Frankincense
   - Narcissus
   - Jasmine
   - Rose
   - Lavender
   - Sandalwood

3. *Stimulates Crown, Third Eye and Etheric Consciousness:*
   - Gum Mastic
   - Musk
   - Henna
   - Myrrh
   - Jasmine
   - Sandalwood
   - Lotus

4. *Facilitates Evolution of Lower Chakra States:*
   - Agarwood
   - Jasmine
   - Amber
   - Rose

5. *Purifies and Cleanses Environment of Discordant Energies:*
   - Agarwood
   - Juniper
   - Cedar
   - Sage
   - Copal
   - Sweet Grass
   - Gum Benzoin

6. *Invokes Benevolent Energies and Spirit Presence:*
   - Amber
   - Gum Mastic
   - Copal
   - Sandalwood
   - Gum Benzoin
   - Sweet Grass

7. *Generates Atmosphere Conducive for Meditation:*
   - Frankincense
   - Musk
   - Sweet Grass
   - Gum Benzoin
   - Myrrh
   - Gum Mastic
   - Sandalwood

CANDLES

As a source of illumination, candles can be very effective in contributing to an atmosphere conducive to Meditation. White candles are particularly effective in transmitting soft, tranquil vibrations, but candles colored to resemble the colors of the different Quartz Crystal varieties used as Meditation subjects can also be very helpful in establishing a mood beneficial to stimulating the visualization and attunement processes. Additionally, scented candles can assist in stimulating conditions of well-being in much the same manner as Incenses and Essential Oils.

FINAL NOTE

It is recommended that The Prayer for Blessing/Invocation, The 23rd Psalm and the Affirmations be memorized, so that the vibrations transmitted by these Statements of Allegiance become a part of your conscious expression of self. Additionally, the words, *"Attune, Balance, Integrate, Ground"*, spoken daily as an audible or silent Mantra in repetitive sets during Meditation serve to help focus and ground mortal consciousness in the reality of God-Conscious Being. By raising mortal resonance rates to more closely approximate the resonance rate of The Council of Twelve, these four words when used together can initiate expanded consciousness states that assist in the assimilation of The Wisdom of One and the conscious application of Divine Truth. It is the attunement to the higher resonance rate of The Yahweh Entity and The Council of Twelve that facilitates man's conscious evolution and ability to reaccess man's inherent, Light-minded nature, which further allows mankind to assume the full responsibility of being true children of The Living God Spirit.

The Meditations that have been described, as well as those that follow, are equally as effective if one chooses to practice them alone or in groups of two or more people with one person leading the group through the Meditation Sequences. In any case, attunement to The Universal One develops as the result of allowing self to understand the deepest truth underlying The Prayer, Psalm and Affirmations, by infusing one's self with Divine Light Vibrations through Crystal Meditations, by allowing and nurturing the unfoldment of the God-self state of being and by allowing the medley of vibrations in your Meditation to evolve and join you as one inspired, resonant vibration that is far greater than the sum of its parts.

When LoveLight Meditation is practiced regularly and Crystal Meditations and Visualization Techniques are included in the daily routine, it is not long before the diligent student realizes that a variety of enhancement conditions have elevated perception modes, as well as stimulated systemic states of conscious well-being. In short, the practice of LoveLight Meditation facilitates man's reaccessing and consciously accepting the God-self, by which mortal man actively communes with The Infinite Body of God. As always, it is recommended that earnest seekers of enlightenment simply allow the journey of life to unfold, without judgements, fears, expectations or demands compromising thoughts and influencing behaviors, and that each seeker allows self to embrace the realities of life with an open, Loving Heart, as therein lies The Grace and Truth that is The Conscience of One.

MEDITATION GUIDELINES

Crystals & Minerals

ADAMITE MEDITATION

Adamite is a Crystalline Zinc Compound found in several parts of the world, including Mexico, Greece and the United States. When attuned to, Adamite allows mankind to break free from conscious thought patterns and third dimension restrictions to soar the cosmos in unfettered astral flight. This Crystal lends itself to almost instantaneous attunement for those soul incarnates who appreciate and welcome the possibilities afforded by astral flight. However, be forewarned that Adamite can in some cases propel one into distant astral states so quickly and with such a sense of integration within other dimensions that disassociation and confusion can result when reintegration into third dimension is attempted. *(For this reason, it is recommended that spheres or eggs of Sheen or Snowflake Obsidian and Smoky Quartz are available for use at the end of this Meditation.)* With adequate preparation, conscious understanding and acceptance of astral sequences, Adamite can prove to be a most illuminating Meditation Partner.

Adamite opens the door to dimensions of consciousness that few mortal incarnates experience on a regular basis. Even though the symbolic references found in dream sequences can be both profound and prophetic, Adamite escorts the willing traveler into the realm of altered consciousness states that rival the drug-induced shamanic journeys undertaken in ancient cultures *(and still practiced today in many parts of the world)*. During these induced astral states, shamans commune with "the dream-time people" who offer wisdom to assist in problem solving. Much the same can happen in Adamite Meditations, as when one travels through different states of expanded consciousness, alternate life forms, as well as symbolic references designed to assist the seeker of enlightenment, are frequently encountered.

1.

To prepare for your Adamite Meditation, select an Adamite formation that will comfortably fit in the palm of your hand. After cleansing and blessing your Adamite, situate yourself in an upright position in a quiet, softly illuminated room that will serve as your Meditation chamber.

2.

Begin your Adamite Meditation by initiating a rhythmic breathing sequence. Breathe deeply, inhaling through your nose, holding the breath for three seconds and slowly exhaling from your mouth. As you inhale, visualize Golden/White Light Vibrations entering your nose, filling your trachea, lungs, chest cavity and heart center with glowing LoveLight Sensations. As you exhale, visualize discordant emotional energy leaving your body in dark, cloudy swirls. Bless yourself and your discordant energy as you cast these unwanted vibrations unto the ether to find Peace. Call upon Yahweh, by The Spirit of Christ, to assist you in the release of your discordant energy.

3.

Now, place your Adamite in your left hand and begin to gaze upon it. Use the index finger of your right hand to stroke your Adamite Crystal and slowly repeat to yourself, *"Attune, Balance, Integrate, Ground."* Repeat these words several times. Now, close your eyes and say to yourself, *"Let the journey begin. Escort me through dimensions of time and space. Through The Grace of Yahweh, let the vision of One unfold. Let the journey begin."* After a short time you will experience warming sensations in your fingers and hands. You will also experience a slight spinning sensation that will develop into a feeling of being lifted from your body. The astral sequence will now commence. Allow yourself to float through layers of consciousness and know that you are being guided to view aspects of Higher Truth. Know that you are being guided to see elements of Universal Truth in a manner that is good and right for your Soul Evolution. Know that you are communing with vibrations whose purpose is to reveal to you The Vision of One. Be at Peace and enjoy the sensations that surround and fill you. Allow yourself to see, feel and exist beyond the limits of time and space. Allow yourself to be as One with all Galactic Creation.

4.

When you are ready to return from your astral flight, reach for your Obsidian and Smoky Quartz Crystals that you have placed near you. Slowly count backwards from ten to one. When you reach one, *REMAIN SEATED AND DO NOT OPEN YOUR EYES.* Now, visualize your body as the trunk of a towering oak tree, your arms as the branches and your legs as the roots. From the bottoms of your feet, the roots extend through the floor and deeply sink into the bosom of Mother Earth. When you have completed this visualization, again count backwards from ten to one. At the count of one, open your eyes and breathe deeply several times. Hold onto your Obsidian and Smoky Quartz Crystals, one in each hand *(hold the Obsidian in your right hand and the Smoky Quartz in your left hand)*, for the next ten to fifteen minutes or until you feel fully integrated in third dimension reality. Now, afford yourself the time to Peacefully reflect upon your Meditation experience.

AMAZONITE MEDITATION

Amazonite amplifies a gentle blue/green ray in The Divine Light Spectrum, whose purpose is to assist mankind in integrating emotional energies of the heart chakra with non-reactionary, benevolent verbal expressions of emotional experiences. This activity, in effect, facilitates the release of discordant and/or painful emotional energies *(memories)* trapped at the heart chakra by encouraging the verbal expression of feelings and memories that form the dissonant energy matrix. Further, Amazonite calms fiery, heart-felt emotions so that motivations and underlying factors contributing to feelings of pain and the need for emotional protection are seen in the truth of reality.

Amazonite is readily available in bead necklaces, cut cabochons and natural specimens, and is priced to accommodate most any budget. *(For this Meditation sequence, it is recommended that a natural specimen of Amazonite be secured from a Rock & Crystal or New Age Shop.)*

1.

To prepare for your Amazonite Meditation, select an Amazonite Crystal that you can comfortably hold in the palm of your hand. Cleanse and bless your Crystal to remove any stored emotional energy that may be present.

2.

To begin your Meditation, situate yourself in a quiet, softly illuminated room and seat yourself in an upright manner. Begin your rhythmic breathing sequence by inhaling deeply through the nose, holding the breath for three seconds and slowly exhaling from the mouth. As you inhale, visualize cleansing Golden/White Light Energy entering your nose, traveling down your trachea, filling your lungs and heart center with glowing LoveLight Sensations. As you exhale, visualize frustration, anger, resentment and pain leaving your body in dark, cloudy swirls of energy. Bless yourself and your discordant energy in The Name of Yahweh, by The Spirit of Christ Jesus, as you cast these disruptive vibrations unto the ether to find Peace.

3.

Pick up your Amazonite Crystal in your left hand and begin to gaze upon it. With the index finger of your right hand, begin to stroke your Crystal and repeat to yourself, *"Attune, Balance, Integrate, Ground."* Repeat these words several times. Soon you may begin to feel warming sensations in your hands, arms and heart chakra. These sensations indicate that the attunement process is beginning to take place.

4.

Now, close your eyes and repeat to yourself, *"Attune to the blue/green ray of Amazonite. Attune. Attune. Attune to the blue/green ray of Amazonite."* Repeat these words several times and allow yourself to merge with the vibrations amplified through your Amazonite Crystal.

5.

Now, visualize a sphere colored with the blue/green ray of Amazonite residing at your heart chakra. Feel the warm, benevolent sensations beginning to rise within you. Feel your heart chakra radiating with the blue/green ray of Amazonite. From the center of the blue/green sphere at your heart chakra, visualize a blue/green beam of Divine Light Vibration that rises up to your throat chakra each time you inhale. Watch as the blue/green beam colors your throat chakra with warm, benevolent sensations. Now, visualize your throat chakra encompassed by a sphere colored with the blue/green ray of Amazonite. Feel the connection between your heart and throat chakra, as you watch the blue/green ray rise from the center of the blue/green sphere at your heart chakra to meet the blue/green sphere at your throat chakra. Allow yourself to experience the calm, cleansing sensations that facilitate Light-minded expression of the emotional energies of your heart chakra.

6.

When you are ready to end your Amazonite Meditation, simply count backwards from ten to one. At the count of one, open your eyes and remain seated. Breathe deeply several times to ensure grounding before you move about. More often than not, you will simply wish to remain seated as you reflect upon the sense of Peace that fills you.

AMBER MEDITATION

Formed from the resin deposits of extinct cone-bearing trees millions of years ago *(during the Oligocene epoch)*, Amber resonates with vibrations of ancient life energy. Technically classified as a fossilized resin and not a mineral, Amber specimens can be found containing preserved twigs, leaves and insects fully intact, illustrating the interface of two Kingdoms: plant and animal. Vibrating with Earth energies that impact upon the navel *(2nd)* chakra, the transition state of Amber demonstrates the cooperative mode achieved by elements of different Kingdoms.

Amber transmits strong facilitating impulses that can literally absorb physical dysfunctions and/or illnesses that center about the navel chakra. It can draw the energy of illnesses from the body and hold the discordant energy within the matrix of the fossilized resin. Amber also impacts upon the nervous system on the cellular level, strengthening and reinforcing nerve tissues to withstand the daily stresses encountered in mortal existence. *(As Amber readily absorbs discordant vibrations when held, frequent cleansing and blessing of your Amber specimen is encouraged.)*

Traditionally, Amber has been used from the Baltic coast to the Caribbean in jewelry making and as a carving medium to fashion fetishes and tools endowed with special curative and protective powers. African and early European cultures were known to fashion necklaces of Amber beads that were used in rituals celebrating man's connection with The Earth Mother. Predating recorded history, mankind has utilized Amber's vibration of life to transcend human frailties and to establish and nurture conscious respect for and connection with the very essence of life upon Mother Earth.

Amber can be purchased today in many appealing forms. From exquisite bead necklaces, earrings, pendants and rings to free-form cabochons and rough, natural specimens, Amber can be found in a form and price range to suit every taste and budget. It should be noted, however, that the finer selections of Amber can be rather expensive, but for the purpose of this Meditation, natural or rough Amber specimens of lower grades will produce results equally acceptable as the results produced by the higher grades of Amber.

1.

To prepare for your Amber Meditation, select an Amber specimen that can comfortably be held in the palm of your hand. Follow the procedure for cleansing and blessing Crystals and Gemstones to be used in Meditation with water and sunlight. Situate yourself in an upright position *(an armless, straight-backed chair is recommended)* in a quiet, softly illuminated room. After a short period, the amount of time required to achieve satisfactory results from this and all other Meditations described in this text may be reduced, because the intuitive and conscious understanding of the attunement process required for the execution of these Meditations becomes second nature to all who diligently apply the procedures outlined.

2.

Now that you are comfortably seated, begin your Meditation with a rhythmic breathing sequence. Breathe deeply, inhaling through your nose, holding the breath for three seconds and slowly exhaling from your mouth. As you inhale, visualize cleansing Golden/White Light Vibrations entering your nose, traveling down your throat, filling your lungs, chest cavity and heart center with warm, radiant, LoveLight Vibrations. As you exhale, visualize discordant energies, stress, tension, frustration, anger, hostility, resentment, leaving your body in dark, cloudy swirls. Bless yourself and your discordant energies in The Name of Yahweh, by The Spirit of Christ Jesus, and cast your discordant vibrations unto the ether to find Peaceful resolution. Continue your rhythmic breathing sequence for three to five minutes or until you feel your body becoming very relaxed.

3.

Pick up your Amber specimen in your left hand and begin to gaze upon it. Notice any internal characteristics that may be present. Visually fix the color of your Amber specimen in your mind. With the index finger of your right hand, begin to stroke your Amber and silently repeat to yourself, *"Attune to the benevolent Earth energy amplified through Amber. Attune. Attune. Attune to the consoling Earth vibrations of Amber."* Repeat these words to yourself several times. Continue to gaze upon your Amber and allow your consciousness to merge with the Amber. Close your eyes and silently say to yourself, *"Attune, Balance, Integrate, Ground."* Repeat these words several times. You may notice that the Amber has become warm in your hand and that there are pulsing sensations in your hands and arm. These are the physical sensations associated with merging and attuning your energy matrix with the energy amplified through the Amber.

4.

Now, place your Amber directly against your navel chakra *(about two inches below the navel)*. Next, visualize the color of your Amber as a sphere slowly rotating clockwise at your navel chakra. Feel the warm, radiant energy that has now taken residence at your navel chakra. See the sphere of Amber expand from your navel chakra to fill your entire abdominal cavity. Feel the warm, glowing LoveLight Sensations, the facilitating vibrations of Amber, that fill you. Allow yourself to be at Peace. Allow yourself to commune with the very essence of life. Allow yourself to be at Peace.

At this time, should there be a physical illness or dysfunction in the area of the abdominal cavity, ask your Amber to absorb the discordant energy by saying, *"In The Name of Yahweh, by The Spirit of Christ Jesus, I beseech thee gentle friend, ancient keeper of life, to absorb the discordant energy troubling me. I ask thee, Amber, to absorb my discordant energy."* Now, place the Amber directly over the area of discomfort and visualize your pain as a cloudy swirl of energy leaving your abdominal area and moving into the Amber. Hold the visualization until you see the last remnant of discordant energy move into the Amber.

5.

When you are ready to terminate your Meditation, simply count backwards from ten to one. When you reach one, open yours eyes and take several deep breaths. Do not be in a hurry to move about. Give yourself as much time as you need to fully integrate into the reality of your Meditation room. If your Amber appears cloudy, do not be alarmed as this is quite commonplace. Simply cleanse and bless your Amber and the discoloration will disappear, as the cloudy appearance is merely the discordant energy the Amber absorbed from you during the Meditation.

AMETHYST MEDITATION

Amethyst Quartz Crystals amplify the soothing, purple ray of The Divine Light Spectrum that enables mankind to calm the conscious mind so that the Wisdom and guidance of the intuitive self can surface. It is by allowing the Wisdom of the intuitive self to rise and become an active part of daily life that mortal man becomes aware of and accepts his innate connection to all things born of Creation. Indeed, The Voice of God speaks in man's own voice and through man's actions as man demonstrates Love, Respect, Compassion and Mercy in his tending of Mother Earth.

Amethyst, along with Citrine, Rose, Smoky and Clear Quartz Crystals form the foundation of Crystalline Consciousness that assist in mankind's journey of Soul Evolution, as these Crystals facilitate the basic opening and aligning of chakras that encourage man to continue along the path of enlightenment. It is the task of Amethyst, however, to supply the all-important ingredient of focus, enabling mankind to clear away the confusion of fast-paced living to perceive the truth of one's reality - without delusion, denial or any ego-facilitating devices coloring one's perceptions. Amethyst allows man to calmly and clearly see that which truly is, so that decisions affecting the very nature of one's existence can be based upon the truth and strength of reality. Further, Amethyst soothes the conscious mind and relaxes nervous tensions resultant from long, stressful days, making it possible to enjoy restful sleep at night.

Amethyst Crystals are found in many parts of the world: Mexico, India, Brazil, Russia and The United States to name a few, but the most spectacular Amethyst Crystals are mined in Uruguay. Uruguayan Amethyst Crystals display a rich, uniform, deep purple color throughout the shaft of the Crystal that amplifies a more vibrant, intense ray than Amethyst Crystals from other regions. Siberian Amethyst, however, is darker than Uruguayan Amethyst and acts to ground mental energies to generate calm, rational, less reactionary behavior patterns. Both Uruguayan and Siberian Amethyst are also sought for their purely spectacular visual appearance.

1.

To prepare for your Amethyst Meditation, select an Amethyst point or cluster that exhibits a deep, pure color. Be sure that the point or cluster that you choose will easily fit in the palm of your hand, then cleanse and bless your Amethyst Meditation Partner.

Before attempting this Meditation, spend a little time with your Amethyst point or cluster to become familiar with its faceting, its color intensity and its shape. As you hold and gaze upon your Amethyst Crystal, allow yourself to begin to sense the vibrations of the purple ray amplified through your Amethyst Crystal. After a time, you may begin to experience tingling or warming sensations in your hands, fingers, arms and third eye chakra (center of forehead between eyebrows). This is the beginning of the process of attunement to The Divine Light Vibrations inherent to the Quartz/Mineral Kingdom, and is the fundamental process underlying all Quartz Crystal Meditations. By attuning to The Divine Light Vibrations amplified through

Quartz Crystals, mankind is able to infuse specific Divine Light Energy into areas of the auric and physical bodies that correspond to a given color within the spectrum of Divine Light Energy. In this case, it is the purple ray of Amethyst that corresponds to and directly impacts upon the third eye center *(6th chakra)*, which is the area that governs man's perceptions of reality.

2.

Select a quiet, softly illuminated room to begin your Meditation. After you are comfortably situated in an upright position, begin your rhythmic breathing sequence by inhaling through the nose, holding the breath for three seconds and slowly exhaling from the mouth. As you inhale, visualize cleansing Golden/White Light Vibrations entering your nose, traveling down your trachea, filling your lungs, chest cavity and heart center with glowing LoveLight Sensations. As you exhale, visualize tensions, frustrations and stresses leaving your body in cloudy swirls of energy. Bless yourself and your discordant vibrations in The Name of Yahweh, by The Spirit of Christ Jesus, as you cast these dissonant vibrations unto the ether to find Peace.

3.

Now, pick up your Amethyst Crystal in your left hand and begin to gaze upon it, drinking in the richness of its deep purple color. Relax and consciously say to yourself, *"Attune to the vibrations of the purple ray. Attune. Attune. Attune to the purple ray of Amethyst."* These statements of attunement should be repeated silently over and over again, until a tingling or warming sensation is experienced at the third eye center. *(Do not be discouraged if the tingling or warming sensations are not produced the first time you attempt this Meditation, as individual differences and readiness result in varying time periods required to produce attunement effects. Be patient and persistent, as your desire for attunement will ultimately allow you to absorb the vibrations amplified through your Amethyst Crystal.)*

After gazing upon your Amethyst Crystal for a time, begin to stroke it with the index finger of your right hand. Close your eyes and envision the purple color of your Amethyst Crystal as a glowing, purple sphere slowly rotating clockwise above your head. Now, watch as the purple sphere slowly descends and penetrates your crown chakra and fills your third eye with the glowing purple ray. If the color of the Amethyst sphere begins to fade, open your eyes immediately and again gaze upon your Crystal. Continue this procedure until you are able to fill your third eye with the purple color of Amethyst and hold the visualization for up to three minutes.

4.

Next, allow the purple sphere to descend along your chakra cord to fill your throat chakra with the purple ray. Now you have the glowing, purple ray of Amethyst soothing both your third eye and throat chakras. If the color begins to fade or you lose the visualization, immediately open your eyes, gaze upon your Amethyst Crystal and begin again.

Follow the same procedure to include the heart center, solar plexus, navel and base chakras. Visualize each of your seven primary chakra centers glowing simultaneously with the deep purple ray of the Amethyst sphere.

From each of the chakra centers that you have colored with the purple sphere, visualize the color of Amethyst spreading to fill up your entire body with the purple ray. Skull, face, neck, shoulders, chest, arms, hands, fingers, abdomen, waist, hips, thighs, knees, lower legs, ankles, feet and toes are all colored with the purple ray of Amethyst. Your body has now become totally permeated by the soothing, purple ray amplified through your Amethyst Crystal, and now you have achieved a blissful state of Tranquility.

As your body glows with the purple ray, visualize the color of Amethyst spreading from your body to engulf the entire room with the purple ray of Amethyst. Look about the room and see that everything, including your physical body, is glowing with the calming, benevolent color of Amethyst.

5.

Hold this visualization for as long as you wish. When you are ready to return to the reality of your Meditation room, simply count backwards from ten to one. At the count of one, slowly open your eyes. Remain seated. Observe how relaxed yet exhilarated you feel. Remain seated. Sense the vibration of the purple ray that remains. Know now that at any time, any place, you can take a moment to envision the purple ray amplified through Amethyst and embrace the clarity of perception that will allow you to negotiate any situation. Arise with an understanding that heretofore has lain dormant within you. Arise with the vision of Light-minded understanding. Arise with the gentle Light of Tranquility and Love radiating in your eyes.

APATITE MEDITATION

Blue Apatite is one of the very best Crystalline Forms to use in cases when stuttering and tension within the throat chakra are present. The gentle vibration that Apatite amplifies slowly opens and stabilizes the energies of the throat chakra. With its soothing blue ray, Apatite also impacts upon and clears rear third eye congestion and calms anxious heart chakra vibrations. (*Rear third eye is the area at the back of the head just above the point at which the skull and neck unite - the occipital bone.*)

Reasonably priced and available at most Rock and Crystal Shops, Apatite is usually sold in rough chunks or small polished slabs, but Apatite beads and other jewelry items are becoming more readily available.

1.

To prepare for your Apatite Meditation, select an Apatite specimen that you can comfortably hold in the palm of your hand. Cleanse and bless your Crystal and situate yourself in a quiet room that is softly illuminated and adopt an upright seating position.

2.

Begin your Meditation by initiating a rhythmic breathing sequence. Inhale deeply through your nose, hold the breath for three seconds and exhale from your mouth. As you inhale, visualize cleansing Golden/White Divine Light Energy filling your lungs, chest cavity and heart center with radiant LoveLight Vibrations. As you exhale, visualize tension and frustration leaving your body in dark, cloudy swirls of discordant energy. Bless yourself and these discordant vibrations in The Name of Yahweh and cast them unto the ether to find Peace.

3.

Now, pick up your Apatite Crystal with your left hand and begin to gaze upon it. Notice the varying intensities of blue found within your Crystal and repeat these words to yourself, *"Attune to the blue ray of Apatite. Attune. Attune. Attune to the blue ray of Apatite."* With the index finger of your right hand gently stroke your Apatite Crystal. Continue your deep breathing and maintain your gaze upon your Crystal. Now, repeat these words to yourself, *"Attune, Balance, Integrate, Ground."* Say these words several times to yourself. After a time you may begin to experience sensations of warmth or tingling in your fingers, hands and arms. You may also experience energy movement in your rear third eye, throat and heart chakras.

At this time, place your Apatite Crystal against your throat chakra with your left hand and hold it in place for up to ten minutes. Allow yourself to experience the soothing vibrations being amplified through your Crystal. Feel the release of tension and stress from your throat chakra that will allow you to express yourself with precision, benevolence and purpose. Allow the blue ray being amplified through your Crystal to bathe your throat chakra with sensations of Peace, balance and The Love of Creation. Allow yourself to feel and commune with The Vibrations of One.

4.

When you are ready to end your Apatite Meditation, simply count backwards from ten to one. At the count of one, breathe deeply, inhaling through the nose and exhaling from the mouth. Open your eyes and remain seated. Reflect upon your Meditation and savor The Divine Light Vibrations with which you have communed.

APOPHYLLITE MEDITATION

Apophyllite is a Hydrated Potassium Calcium Silicate with a cubic or octahedral appearance that ranges in color from green to yellow or with shades of pink, white and colorless. Found in several parts of the world, Apophyllite of the green, white and colorless varieties from India is presently the most viable source for the western market.

As a tool of Higher Consciousness, Apophyllite aids mortal evolution by stimulating the conscious acceptance of the etheric body's acknowledgment and execution of Precepts of Universal Truth and Divine Will. This process and state of conscious acceptance is the result of Apophyllite's assistance in sharpening mortal perceptions of Spiritual Realities by dissolving or penetrating layers of interference and resistance associated with physical realities and the linear thought process. Apophyllite impacts the subtle aspects of astral perceptions that facilitate the third eye and heart chakra's acceptance of the definitive expressions of Universal Consciousness, which in turn facilitates the evolution and ascension of mortal consciousness in The Light of The One. Additionally, Apophyllite stimulates nonverbal, intuitive understanding of those aspects of evolved consciousness that are Universally accepted as "good and right" for all things born of Creation, making it no longer necessary to think about or ponder the available choices of behaviors to suit a particular life-condition; rather, one simply "knows" at the heart-centered level the behaviors of conscience one needs to engage to impact The Greater Good.

Frequently, Apophyllite is found in deposits with other Minerals, such as Prehnite and Stilbite, that augment and amplify the properties of Apophyllite. Apophyllite/Prehnite combinations amplify the experience and comprehension of Divine Truth by stimulating Cosmic Illumination and increasing the instances of "Intuitive Knowingness". Apophyllite/Stilbite formations stimulate prolonged and intensified astral states, while simultaneously transmitting intuitive understanding that clarifies and puts into perspective the relative importance of the temporal nature of physical reality as opposed to the limitless nature of Divine Wisdom.

1.

To begin your Apophyllite Meditation, seat yourself in a comfortable upright position in a quiet, dimly lit room. Hold your Apophyllite in the left hand and begin to gaze upon it, gently stroking the Crystal with the index finger of your right hand.

2.

Now, close your eyes and begin rhythmic breathing, inhaling deeply through the nose, holding the breath for three seconds and slowly exhaling from the mouth. As you engage the rhythmic breathing sequence, silently repeat these words several times, *"Attune, Balance, Integrate, Ground"*. Allow self to relax and continue your rhythmic breathing.

3.

Now, slowly raise your Apophyllite Crystal and place it against your third eye with your left hand. Place your right hand over your left hand. Hold the Crystal in place for up to three minutes. While holding the Apophyllite against your third eye, slowly and silently repeat these words, *"Attune, Balance, Integrate, Ground. In The Name of Yahweh, By The Spirit of The Christ, let me attune to the vibrations of Apophyllite."* Repeat these statements three times.

Soon you will begin to feel light-headed, with warm sensations filling your chakra cord. These feelings indicate that the astral or expanded consciousness phase has begun. Relax and allow self to experience that which is simply beyond words. Relax and allow self to experience the moment of Illumination in The Light of The One Infinite Creator.

4.

When you are ready to end your Apophyllite Meditation, count backwards from ten to one. At the count of one, slowly open your eyes, REMAIN SEATED and breathe deeply. Remain seated and allow yourself ample time to fully reintegrate and ground within third dimension before moving about. Reflect upon your Meditation and allow self to understand that in Truth, indeed, *"All Is As One"*.

ATACAMITE MEDITATION

Atacamite, the benevolent coordinator, has as its purpose the directive to assist mankind in establishing a balance of emotional states, and to aid in integrating Etheric Constructs of Peace and Tranquility with emotional expressions, thereby facilitating the moment when Divine and "Earth-bound" exist as one. Found in deposits with veins of copper-related minerals *(especially Chrysocolla)* in Chile, Atacamite aims to release mortal man from left brain/right brain conflicts and gently sets the stage for the cooperative union of masculine and feminine vibrations. Atacamite offers itself as a tool in man's evolutionary journey toward The Wisdom of One by interfacing drives of aggression, compulsions for survival and conditioned behaviors designed for self-service with realities of Etheric Truth. With the values of Patience, Compassion, Wisdom, Mercy, Serenity and Love in the service to all Creation as a part of human motivation and purpose, mankind can develop and display the Light-minded characteristics that personify The God Spirit.

1.

To prepare for your Atacamite Meditation, select a natural specimen that you can comfortably hold in your hand. Cleanse and bless your Atacamite and situate yourself in a softly illuminated, quiet room in an upright position.

2.

Begin your Meditation with a rhythmic breathing sequence by inhaling deeply through your nose, holding the breath for three seconds and exhaling from your mouth. As you inhale, visualize radiant Golden/White Light Vibrations entering your nose, traveling down your trachea, filling your lungs, chest cavity and heart center with glowing LoveLight Energy. As you exhale, visualize discordant energy leaving your body in dark, cloudy swirls. Bless yourself and your discordant vibrations in The Name of Yahweh, by The Spirit of Christ Jesus, as you cast this dissonant energy unto the ether to find Peace. Relax and begin to gaze upon your Atacamite Crystal.

3.

As you gaze upon your Atacamite Crystal, drinking in the sparkling, blue/green energy it amplifies, allow yourself to become one with your Crystal. Stroke your Atacamite with the index finger of your right hand and repeat to yourself, *"Attune to the blue/green ray of Atacamite. Attune. Attune. Attune to the blue/green ray of Atacamite."* Repeat these words several times. Now, visually fix the color of Atacamite in your mind and close your eyes and repeat to yourself, *"Attune, Balance, Integrate, Ground."* Repeat these words three times. You will probably have experienced tingling sensations along your chakra cord by this time, so continue to relax and once again repeat to yourself, *"Attune to the blue/green ray of Atacamite. Attune. Attune. Attune to the blue/green ray of Atacamite."*

4.

Now, visualize Atacamite as a sparkling, blue/green sphere slowly rotating clockwise above your head. From the center of the blue/green sphere, visualize a blue/green beam that emerges and slowly travels down to penetrate your crown chakra and third eye center. Watch as the blue/green Atacamite beam continues downward through your throat chakra, energizing you. See your chakra cord merge with the blue/green beam, as the beam travels to color your entire chakra cord with the blue/green ray. See your heart center, solar plexus, navel and base chakras infused with the blue/green ray of Atacamite. Feel the sense of exhilaration and integration that fills you. Now, visualize the blue/green ray of Atacamite spreading from your chakra centers and chakra cord to fill your entire body with the benevolent blue/green ray of Atacamite. Feel the sense of absolute calm and freedom from encumbering energy systems that fills you. Should visionary sequences commence at this time, allow yourself to see and understand the message being transmitted to you. Allow yourself to be at Peace and to fully resolve any energy imbalances that may exist within your primary chakra system.

5.

When you are ready to return from your Atacamite Meditation, simply count backwards from ten to one. At the count of one, open your eyes and breathe deeply several times. Reflect upon your Meditation experience and observe the sense of Tranquility that fills you. Be at Peace within The Light of One, and know that you have communed with the energies of the Universe that balance the conscience of the sage.

AVENTURINE

Aventurine combines the deep green vibration of Mother Earth with the golden ray of Etheric Consciousness, represented by the golden Pyrite flecks found within Aventurine's green Crystalline matrix. Aventurine works to channel energies to assist mankind in achieving balance both physically and emotionally. Further, Aventurine directs crown chakra vibrations into the heart chakra, such that conscious understanding, both intellectually and emotionally, of the Healing Facilitation mode can occur. This is to say that Aventurine assists mankind in comprehending the dynamics of energies of facilitation on an intellectual and emotional level, and goes one step further by guiding us in assimilating the actual transforming, nurturing Mother Earth Vibrations on both the conscious and the intuitive levels.

Aventurine varies in color and color intensity from the palest apple or lime green tones to shades of green that resemble meadow grass and the darker greens of foliage plant leaves such as the kentia palm, chinese evergreen and the darkest of african violet leaves. Aventurine is found in shades of orange and yellow as well, but for purposes of Meditation, it is recommended that Aventurine specimens of the medium to dark green varieties be selected.

1.

To prepare for your Aventurine Meditation, select an Aventurine Crystal that appeals to your senses and comfortably rests in the palm of your hand. *(Even though Aventurine can be purchased in cut and polished pyramids, obelisks, eggs, cubes and natural or tumbled specimens, it is recommended that an Aventurine sphere be selected for use in this Meditation.)*

After cleansing and blessing your Aventurine sphere, situate yourself in a quiet, softly illuminated room and sit in an upright position. Pick up your Aventurine sphere in your left hand and begin to gaze upon it. Observe the unique pattern that the Pyrite flecks make and notice the harmony of the gold tones set against the warm, rich green shade of your Aventurine Crystal.

2.

Begin your rhythmic breathing sequence by inhaling deeply through the nose, holding the breath for three seconds and exhaling from the mouth. As you inhale, visualize radiant, cleansing Golden/White Light Energy filling your lungs, chest cavity and heart center with warm LoveLight Vibrations. As you exhale, visualize tension and stress, frustration and anger leaving your body in dark, cloudy swirls of discordant energy. Bless yourself and your discordant, counter-productive vibrations in The Name of Yahweh and cast these discordant vibrations unto the ether to find Peaceful resolution.

3.

With the index finger of your right hand begin to stroke your Aventurine sphere as you repeat these words to yourself: *"Attune to the benevolent green ray of Aventurine. Attune. Attune.*

Attune to the benevolent green ray of Aventurine." Repeat these words to yourself several times. Intensify your gaze upon the sphere and continue your rhythmic breathing for three to five minutes.

You may now begin to experience energy movements in your hands, fingers and arms. You may also begin to experience sensations of warmth or tingling in your chest at your heart chakra. Now, repeat to yourself, *"Attune, Balance, Integrate, Ground."* Close your eyes and again repeat to yourself, *"Attune, Balance, Integrate, Ground."* Your breathing will have become shallow by this time.

4.

Now, place your right hand beneath your left hand and cradle your Aventurine sphere. Raise the sphere to your chest and place it against your heart chakra. Hold your Aventurine against your heart chakra for five to ten minutes. As you hold the Aventurine sphere against your heart chakra, visualize the nurturing green ray of Aventurine as a rich green sphere filling your heart chakra with radiant energy. Visualize the green ray of Aventurine as it slowly rotates clockwise with benevolent LoveLight Vibration intent upon imparting the Blessings of The Universal One to every fiber of your being.

Now, visualize a golden ray above your head that enters your crown chakra and travels down your chakra cord to your heart center. When the golden ray reaches your heart center, watch as the golden ray delicately swirls and commingles with the green sphere. Watch as the golden ray gently enhances the Earthy, green sphere, adding touches of Light-mindedness in golden wisps of consciousness. Watch and feel as you become filled with a sense of Divine Comprehension of the Universal

Vibrations of Healing Facilitation. Allow yourself to sense the non-verbal Wisdom rising within you. Allow yourself to sense the facilitation modalities alive within you. Allow yourself to sense The LoveLight Vibrations of One.

5.

When you are ready to return to the reality of your Meditation room, simply count backwards from ten to one. When you reach one, open your eyes, breathe deeply several times, inhaling through your nose and exhaling from your mouth, and know that you are fully grounded in third dimension reality. Savor the warm, glowing sensations that fill you. Reflect upon your experience of merging with your Aventurine sphere. Look upon your Aventurine sphere, as it almost seems to be smiling at you, and know that the facilitating vibrations of Mother Earth and The Light of The Infinite One are alive within you.

AZULICITE MEDITATION

Azulicite Meditation assists the Healing Facilitator or anyone involved in hands-on bodywork in maintaining or regaining his/her proper energy alignment after taxing sessions. Azulicite's activity impacts upon the meridian chakras to align energy systems that have been strained as the result of prolonged energy transmissions and/or transmutations. The translucent Moonstone-like appearance of Azulicite amplifies a Light Vibration that revitalizes, balances and integrates the meridian chakras to reduce the physical stress of facilitation and bodywork.

1.

To prepare for your Azulicite Meditation, select eight (8) small pieces of Azulicite Crystal and cleanse and bless your Azulicite in the prescribed manner. Since the activity of Azulicite begins as soon as the Crystals are handled, and since it is not necessary to prepare for a standard Meditation sequence, this Meditation can be performed even under the most distracting, adverse conditions.

To begin your Meditation, seat yourself and place one piece of Azulicite between each of your fingers on both hands. Rest your hands on your upper thighs with the palms open and facing up. Close your eyes and say to yourself, *"Attune, Balance, Integrate, Ground."* Repeat these words several times to yourself. In a matter of moments, you will begin to feel tingling sensations working to align your energy matrix. Hold this position for five to ten minutes to achieve the maximum results.

3.

Now, remove the Azulicite Crystals from between your fingers and place the Crystals between your toes. Again say to yourself, *"Attune, Balance, Integrate, Ground."* Very quickly you will feel surges of energy in your lower extremities moving to balance and align your energy systems. Hold the Azulicite Crystals in place for five to ten minutes.

To assist in the alignment of your energy systems in only sixty seconds, place Azulicite Crystals between the fingers of your left hand. Now, with your palm open and facing up, place another Azulicite Crystal upon your left wrist and hold it in position with the index finger of your right hand. Repeat to yourself, *"Attune, Balance, Integrate, Ground."* By the time these words have been repeated three times, you will have experienced shifts in your energy matrix designed to achieve alignment.

CALCITE MEDITATION

Calcite is one of the most diverse and important groups of Minerals that can be attuned to by mortal man to stimulate and reinforce the process of Spiritual Evolution. Calcite occurs in natural rhomboid shapes, finger-like growths, crystallized formations and block deposits in at least nine different color varieties, each of which bears specific significance to the function of mental/etheric activities. Calcite offers mankind assistance in the integration of the etheric and mental bodies, so that comprehension of Divine Wisdom can take place within the framework of third dimension realities. Calcite fingers that are usually tabular in structure are available in most color varieties and are excellent tools for bridging the etheric and mental bodies. Properties of the nine most commonly encountered Calcite forms are as follows:

BLUE CALCITE: aids in stimulating clarity in the conscious thought process, which enables clear transmission of Etheric Wisdom in the spoken word

BROWN CALCITE: reinforces expressions of Etheric consciousness through base chakra activities

CLEAR OPTICAL CALCITE (Iceland Spar): aids in expanding the crown chakra, thereby energizing the auric system;

intensifies mental capacities; provides clear transmission of Divine Light Vibration that enables the integration of Etheric Consciousness with mental activities

GREEN CALCITE: aids in soothing overwrought mental faculties; aids in transforming burnout syndrome; calms the mental/emotional body to assist in the assimilation of Absolute Truth

HONEY CALCITE: aids in the transmission of Etheric Consciousness into the dynamics of navel center function; impacts upon physical body *(organ system associated with the navel chakra)* by stimulating the transmutation of dysfunctional, debilitating memory systems; essential stone for assisting in the transmutation of blockages resultant from mental/emotional dysfunctions *(inability to successfully compete and excel in accordance with societal conditioning)* associated with the navel center

MANGO CALCITE: aids in the integration of Etheric Wisdom with third dimension behavior modes *(crown to navel)*; helps to integrate elements of higher self

SALMON CALCITE: aids in the integration of the etheric body with the mental and physical bodies; aids in balancing and harmonizing the elements of self

STRAWBERRY CALCITE: transmute strength and conviction of Etheric Wisdom along chakra cord to facilitate expressions of Godliness in daily behaviors; integrates aspects of higher self to facilitate dynamic understanding of Etheric Truth, as evidenced by conscionable thought and behavior patterns; impacts energy states from crown to upper base chakra regions; acts to enhance oxygenation of blood, thereby increasing physical stamina and endurance, while stimulating mental alertness, focus and assertiveness in implementing behaviors of Light-minded Conscience

WHITE CALCITE: aids in improving the conscious memory process; functions to enhance episodes of astral travel and to integrate elements of Higher Truth into the conscious mind

1.

To prepare for your Calcite Meditation, first contemplate the various Calcite colors and forms to determine which ones are most applicable to your immediate needs. Handle as many shapes and colors as possible and allow your intuition to guide you in your selection. It is recommended, however, that you select a Clear Optical Calcite specimen *(rhomboid shape)* as one of your Crystals, for these Crystals open the way *(stimulate the crown chakra)* for the assimilation of energy vibrations from the etheric self.

2.

After cleansing and blessing your Calcite Crystals, situate yourself in a dimly lit, quiet room in an upright position. Begin your rhythmic breathing sequence by inhaling deeply through the nose and exhaling from the mouth. As you inhale, visualize cleansing Golden/White Light Vibrations entering your nose, filling your lungs, chest cavity and heart chakra. As you exhale, visualize tension and stress, frustration and anger leaving your body in dark, cloudy swirls of discordant energy. Bless your discordant vibrations in The Name of Yahweh and cast these discordant energies unto the ether to find Peace. Continue your rhythmic breathing for three to five minutes or until you feel your body becoming relaxed.

3.

Now, pick up your Calcite Crystal in your left hand and begin to gaze upon it. Take the index finger of your right hand and gently stroke the Crystal. Say to yourself, *"Attune to the vibrations of Calcite. Attune. Attune. Attune to the vibrations of Calcite."* After a time, you may begin to feel energy movement in your hands, fingers and arms, and you may also experience energy movement at your crown, third eye and heart chakras.

4.

Now, with your left hand, place your Calcite Crystal against your crown chakra for three to five minutes. While holding the Calcite in place, say to yourself, *"In The Name of Yahweh, let The Truth of Etheric Wisdom fill my consciousness."* Now, move your Calcite to rest against your third eye and say, *"Attune, Balance, Integrate, Ground."* Repeat these words three times. Then once again say to yourself, *"Attune to the vibrations of Calcite."* (*Your breathing will have become quite shallow by this time.*) Relax and allow your energy matrix to attune to The Divine Light Vibrations amplified through your Calcite Crystal.

5.

When you are ready to return to the reality of your Meditation chamber, slowly count backwards from ten to one. At the count of one, *REMAIN SEATED AND DO NOT OPEN YOUR EYES.* Now, visualize your body as the trunk of a majestic oak tree, your arms as the tree's branches and your legs as the roots. From the bottoms of your feet, see the roots pass through the floor and anchor themselves into the heart of Mother Earth. When you have completed this visualization, again count backwards from ten to one. At the count of one, open your eyes and breathe deeply several times, knowing that you are firmly grounded in third dimension reality.

CELESTITE MEDITATION

Celestite Crystals amplify the gentle, pale blue ray of The Divine Light Spectrum that enhances the communication mode of the throat *(5th)* chakra. With the directive to assist its user in traversing levels of Higher Consciousness in order to glean Constructs of Absolute Truth and to express acquired astral knowledge through the spoken word, Celestite comes to mankind as a willing companion eager to assist its user to spread his/her wings and fly amongst the stars. Celestite functions as more than just an enhancer of astral travel, as indeed Celestite is the catalyst for many soul incarnates who have reached the moment of readiness to shed the shackles of mortal consciousness and explore the realms of the Universe - those Light-minded souls who are ready to release from the restrictions of third dimension reality and soar upon wings of pale blue Light to greet the Galactic Creations of The Infinite One.

Celestite Crystals can be found in many parts of the world, but the most exquisite Celestite specimens to date have come from Madagascar. Not only does Madagascan Celestite display a richer, more appealing shade of blue, but more importantly, Madagascan Celestite is bursting with life - with a brilliance, clarity and luster unparalleled by other Celestite deposits.

Commanding slightly higher prices, Madagascan Celestite is worth the extra expense, because The Divine Light Vibration amplified through these Crystals is more pure and consequently more dynamic. Natural Crystals and clusters of Celestite come in a variety of sizes and grades, so there will be a Celestite specimen that will meet the needs of most everyone.

1.

To prepare for your Celestite Meditation, select a natural Crystal or cluster of Celestite. Care is advised in the cleansing of Celestite clusters, because excessive washing can cause the clay-like base of many clusters to dissolve, leaving a group of separate Crystals instead of a cluster. Now, situate yourself in an upright position in a quiet, softly illuminated room. Pick up your Celestite Crystal and begin to gaze upon it.

2.

Begin your rhythmic breathing sequence by inhaling deeply through the nose, holding the breath for three seconds and slowly exhaling from the mouth. As you inhale, visualize glowing, cleansing Golden/White Light Vibrations entering your nose, traveling down your trachea, filling your lungs, chest cavity and heart chakra. As you exhale, visualize discordant energy leaving your body in dark, cloudy swirls of energy. Bless yourself and your discordant vibrations in The Name of Yahweh, by The Spirit of Christ Jesus, as you cast these discordant vibrations unto the ether to find Peaceful resolution.

3.

With the index finger of your right hand begin to stroke your Celestite Crystal. Your breathing will have become shallow by this time, as you become more and more relaxed. Intensify your gaze upon your Celestite, observing the color intensity and the nature of the crystallization that your Celestite displays. Now, silently repeat to yourself, *"Attune to the vibrations of Celestite. Attune. Attune. Attune to the blue ray of Celestite."* Repeat these words several times. Now, close your eyes and silently repeat to yourself, *"Attune, Balance, Integrate, Ground."* Again repeat to yourself, *"Attune, Balance, Integrate, Ground."*

4.

Now, visualize the color of Celestite as a large sphere hovering six inches above your head. You may have begun to experience energy movements in your hands and fingers, and a warm, tingling sensation may have begun in your third eye and throat chakras. Now, watch the light blue sphere of Celestite above your head as it slowly moves down to penetrate your crown chakra, engulfing your third eye and throat chakras. Now, your entire head and neck are within the gentle blue ray of the Celestite sphere. Feel the sense of Peace as you float within the Tranquil blue ray of Celestite. Allow yourself to take flight and soar as you visualize your consciousness merging with the blue sphere of Celestite. Allow yourself the freedom and beauty of galactic flight. Allow yourself to be One with all things of The God's Creation.

5.

When you are ready to return to third-dimension reality, simply count backwards from ten to one. When you reach one, *DO NOT OPEN YOUR EYES AND REMAIN SEATED.* Now, visualize your body as the trunk of a majestic oak tree, your arms as the branches and your legs as the roots. See the roots of the tree extending beyond the bottoms of your feet through the floor and holding fast within the bosom of Mother Earth. When you have completed this visualization, again count backwards from ten to one. When you reach one, open your eyes and breathe deeply several times. Relax and reflect upon your journey. Do not force yourself to remember details. Remain calm and you will remember the essential elements that you experienced during your Celestite Meditation.

CHRYSOCOLLA MEDITATION

The gentle, Compassionate, light blue ray of Chrysocolla amplifies a balancing vibration that soothes overwrought emotional states. Frequently, when hormonal imbalances resultant from menstruation and/or menopause occur, Chrysocolla can lend a comforting vibration that will assist in calming the emotional and physical distress. Additionally, Chrysocolla aids in counterbalancing aggressive energies of the male consciousness, allowing and encouraging the male of the species to contact and utilize inherent feminine energies, thereby developing a more balanced, integrated, functional energy matrix. Chrysocolla gently works upon both the physical and emotional bodies to usher in states of balance and harmony, and helps to guide the dedicated student of Light-mindedness toward Peace and an understanding of The One.

Mined in several locations around the world, Chrysocolla is usually found in association with other copper-related minerals such as Turquoise, Azurite and/or Malachite. Chrysocolla spheres, eggs and free-form polished slabs, as well as pendants, rings, necklaces and earrings are becoming more and more available on the retail market at affordable prices. As the need for the blue ray of Chrysocolla further manifests upon the Earth Plane, more soul incarnates will be guided to utilize the vibrations amplified through this benevolent stone.

1.

To prepare for your Chrysocolla Meditation, select a natural or polished Chrysocolla form that appeals to your senses. Cleanse and bless your Chrysocolla beforehand, so that you can quickly settle into your Meditation mode.

2.

Situate yourself in a quiet room that is softly illuminated and adopt an upright, seated position. Begin your rhythmic breathing sequence by inhaling deeply through the nose, holding the breath for three seconds and exhaling from the mouth. As you inhale, visualize cleansing, radiant Golden/White Light Vibrations entering your nose, filling your lungs, chest cavity and heart center. As you exhale, visualize stress and tension, frustration and anger leaving your body in dark, cloudy swirls of discordant energy. Bless yourself and your discordant vibrations in The Name of Yahweh and cast these counterproductive, debilitating vibrations unto the ether to find Peaceful resolution. Continue your rhythmic breathing for three to five minutes or until you feel your body has become completely relaxed.

3.

Now, pick up your Chrysocolla Crystal in your left hand and begin to gaze upon it. With the index finger of your right hand gently stroke the Crystal, as you repeat to yourself, *"Attune to the vibrations of Chrysocolla. Attune. Attune. Attune to the gentle blue ray of Chrysocolla."* After a short time, you may begin to register energy movement in your fingers, hands and arms, and you may also experience energy movement in your third eye center, throat and heart chakras. *(Energy movement is defined as tingling or sensations of heat or throbbing, pulsating sensations that occur in any part of the physical body and especially at and between chakra centers.)*

4.

Now, visualize the color of Chrysocolla in a glowing blue sphere at your third eye center. See the gentle light blue of Chrysocolla fill your third eye with warm, comforting vibrations. Raise your Chrysocolla with your left hand and place it against your third eye for up to five minutes. Feel Chrysocolla's motivation for balance and Peace, as balance and Peace also become the guiding motivation for your third eye consciousness.

5.

Next, while holding the color of Chrysocolla at your third eye center, visualize Chrysocolla as a warm, blue sphere moving to your throat chakra. Now, move the Chrysocolla from your third eye to rest against your throat chakra. Feel the benevolent, comforting blue ray of Chrysocolla as it soothes any discordant energy associated with verbal expression. See the blue ray of Chrysocolla fill your throat chakra with sensations of Peace.

6.

Now, maintain the visualization of Chrysocolla's blue ray as a warm sphere at both your third eye and throat chakras. Now, also visualize Chrysocolla as a blue sphere of gentle energy at your heart chakra. Move the Chrysocolla Crystal from your throat chakra to your heart center. Feel the calm that permeates you. Feel the blue ray of Chrysocolla as it brings Harmony to your senses. Now, connect the three spheres of Chrysocolla by sending a blue beam from the center of the sphere at your third eye center down through the center of the sphere at your throat chakra and allow the blue beam to continue down from your throat chakra to become one with your heart chakra. Hold this visualization for as long as you desire, and marvel in the absolute sense of Harmony and Peace you have attained. Feel yourself radiate with a gentle assurance that balance and Serenity are birthright precepts of all things born of Creation. See yourself as one fully integrated child of God's Mercy and know that indeed you are part of The Infinite Body of God.

7.

When you are ready to terminate your Meditation, simply count backwards from ten to one and open your eyes. Know that you are grounded in third dimension reality, and that the sense of comfort and Peace that fills you is yours whenever you choose to experience it.

CITRINE QUARTZ MEDITATION

Citrine Quartz Crystals amplify the golden yellow ray of the crown chakra to aid in grounding the purpose of Divine Will into the navel chakra, thereby assisting each soul incarnate in applying "Godliness" to Earthly activities. Many times mortal consciousness can be directed, if not consumed, by the drive toward material acquisition. The need and/or compulsion for possessions and property is behavior orchestrated by the ego and finds expression through the navel center in mankind's perpetual quest to acquire more and more "things".

Citrine offers mankind the opportunity to transmute ego-facilitating patterns and to learn to walk upon Mother Earth with gentle footsteps, acknowledging and treating all life born of Creation with Respect, Love, Patience and Understanding. That is, Citrine assists mankind in evolving to the point where it is clear that serving the needs of his/her brethren and Mother Earth is far more productive than seeking personal gratification and the aggrandizement of self. Citrine Quartz affords those who attune to its vibrations the enlightened perception that life on Earth is a Divine experience that is to be enjoyed and accepted with integrity, humility, joy, conviction and wonder.

Natural Citrine Quartz Crystals occur in shades of yellow to rich golden yellow tones, but heat treatments of these Crystals extend the natural color spectrum to hues of orange and brown. Citrine amplifies vibrations of Higher Consciousness that impact upon man's daily activities, offering mankind a most dynamic tool with which to integrate elements of Universal Law into the physical plane. Occasionally, Citrine and Amethyst can be found within the same Quartz Crystal. Ametrine, as these Crystals are called, make excellent Meditation Partners also, for Ametrine harmonizes the purple ray of third eye clarity with the golden yellow ray of the crown chakra to facilitate enlightened third dimension expressions of self through the navel center.

1.

To begin your Citrine Meditation, select a Citrine Crystal that has been cleansed and blessed. Situate yourself in a softly illuminated, quiet room in an upright position. Begin your rhythmic breathing sequence by inhaling through the nose and slowly exhaling from the mouth. As you inhale, visualize cleansing Golden/White Light Energy entering your nose, filling your lungs, chest cavity and heart center. As you exhale, visualize tension, frustration, anger and stress leaving your body in dark, cloudy swirls of energy. Bless yourself and these discordant vibrations in The Name of Yahweh, as you cast your discordant energies unto the ether to find Peace.

2.

Now, pick up your Citrine Crystal in your left hand and begin to gaze upon it. Observe the internal elements of your Crystal, the subtle color changes, rainbows, mists and swirls. Say to yourself, *"Attune to the vibrations of Citrine. Attune. Attune. Attune to the golden yellow ray of Citrine."* Repeat these statements several times. Before long, you may experience a warming or a tingling sensation in your hand, fingers and arm. You may also begin to feel energy surges at your crown and navel chakras. *(Your breathing will have become shallow at this point.)*

3.

Now, close your eyes and visualize the color of Citrine in a glowing sphere above your head. Slowly raise your Crystal and place it against your third eye center. Visualize the Citrine sphere above your head radiating and beaming a golden yellow ray from your crown chakra down the center line of your body *(your chakra cord)* to your navel center. *(It is good to place your right hand on the navel center to aid in the visualization placement.)* Now, visualize a glowing sphere both above your head and at your navel center connected by the golden yellow beam. Hold this visualization for five minutes or for as long as you can. When you have a clear visualization of the two spheres connected by the golden yellow beam, repeat these words to yourself, *"Attune, Balance, Integrate, Ground."* Repeat these words three times while the visualization is clear. When you are no longer able to hold the visualization, simply release yourself from the Meditation by breathing deeply several times, then open your eyes.

By practicing Citrine Quartz Meditations, each soul incarnate can intimately learn how to apply The Divine Light Vibrations of the crown chakra to his/her physical world. It is not always a matter of consciously or verbally understanding the elements of Ethereal Reasoning; rather, it is far more important to intuitively comprehend that which is "good and right". Citrine Meditation enables mortal man to develop the intuitive voice that speaks over and above societal conditioning and emotional traumas that impede the expression of Light-mindedness. Citrine Quartz Crystals offer the evolving consciousness of man the opportunity to connect with and exemplify the Divine attributes of the etheric self.

DIOPTASE MEDITATION

With one of the most strikingly brilliant emerald-green displays encountered in either the Plant or Mineral Kingdom, Crystalline Dioptase stimulates a sense of playfulness and joyful celebration that facilitates the release of self-importance, as well as aids in transmuting the driving desire for accomplishment sometimes associated with job performance and the expectations of self. With the inspired purpose of lessening the burden of illusion of self that man frequently and unwittingly creates, Dioptase joins several other Crystals (such as Phantom Quartz, Imperial Topaz and Elestial Quartz to name a few) as conscionable tools to assist in the transformation of ego-consciousness and to aid in the subsequent evolution of God-Conscious Being.

Dioptase is a Hydrous Copper Silicate Crystal found in Namibia, Chile and Zaire, and recently Dioptase has been exported from states of the former Soviet Union. Available from Crystal Shops and New Age Retailers, Dioptase is costly, but its high potential for offering assistance in the journey of Soul Evolution well warrants the expense.

1.

To begin your Dioptase Meditation, first seat yourself in an upright position, in a dimly lit, quiet room. Hold your Dioptase in your left hand and rest your left hand facing palm up in the palm of your right hand. Place both hands in your lap. Begin to gaze upon your Dioptase (if necessary, bring the Dioptase Crystal up to eye level). Allow yourself to relax and absorb the wonderfully radiant, emerald-green ray of Dioptase. Relax.

2.

Now, begin a rhythmic breathing sequence by inhaling deeply through the nose, holding the breath for three seconds and slowly exhaling from the mouth. Close your eyes, and as you continue the rhythmic breathing, silently repeat these words several times, *"Attune, Balance, Integrate, Ground"*.

3.

After a short time, open your eyes and once again gaze upon your Dioptase for up to 90 seconds. Now, close your eyes and visualize the emerald-green color of Dioptase filling your heart chakra with waves of warm, Loving Energy. Feel the emerald-green ray of Dioptase as it gently fills your heart chakra with warm sensations of joyful understanding that facilitates the release of the self-imposed burden of performance. Feel the emerald-green ray of Dioptase as it assists you in allowing self to experience the joyful exuberance and wonderment of life. Feel the emerald-green ray of Dioptase as it guides you toward embracing self and all things born of Creation in the benevolent arms of Love and Peace.

4.

When you are ready to disengage from your Dioptase Meditation, simply count backwards from ten to one. At the count of one, open your eyes, breathe deeply and reflect upon your Meditation. Allow yourself ample time to assimilate the vibrations with which you have communed, and feel the comfort and assurance that makes it possible for you to allow all things to simply "be".

ELESTIAL QUARTZ MEDITATION

Upon initial observation, Elestial Quartz Crystals clearly display characteristics that identify them as truly unique members of the Quartz/Mineral Kingdom. Elestial Quartz Crystals have fully terminated faces over the entire surface of the Crystal, and are further identified by their layered, Crystalline appearance. Also known as Cathedral or Alligator Quartz, Elestial Crystals are not indigenous to Mother Earth, but were transported into the Earth Plane from the galactic reaches to aid in mankind's evolving consciousness. Many of these Crystals show unmistakable signs of having been "fired", as evidenced by charred, blackened areas of the Crystals resultant from their entry into the Earth's atmosphere.

Elestial Quartz Crystals' distinctive, layered formation is analogous to the layers of human consciousness, wherein reside the keys to understanding the unfoldment of one's Earthly journey. By attuning to the vibrations of and merging one's consciousness with the structure of Elestial Quartz Crystals, one is assisted in stripping away the layers of conditioning that impede the true identification and understanding of self. Elestial Crystals stand ready to aid those soul incarnates who seek the vision of pure self, unencumbered by societal constraints, unshackled by emotional scar tissue and unfettered by false pride and self-importance. These Crystals strip away layer after layer of ego-facilitating motivations to reveal the bare facts, thereby enabling the individual to be consciously aware of those elements of one's makeup in need of transmutation.

(NOTE: *It must be stated here that discretion should be exercised in engaging in Elestial Quartz Meditation. Adequate groundwork must be laid to understand the dynamics of one's core motivations, as Elestial Quartz Crystals can be ruthless in stripping away and revealing layers of consciousness. It is therefore advised that the LoveLight Invocation, Affirmations and Prayers, as well as Amethyst, Rose, Citrine and Smoky Quartz Meditations are practiced prior to engaging in Elestial Quartz Meditations.)*

1.

Select an Elestial Quartz Crystal that seems to draw your attention, guiding you to pick it up and handle it. Allow your intuition to guide you in your selection, as you will be directed toward the Crystal that is right for you. *(Of course, price consideration may also be an issue, as some of the larger Elestial Crystals are rather expensive.)*

After cleansing your Crystal, situate yourself in an upright position in a quiet, softly illuminated room. Begin your relaxation with rhythmic breathing, inhaling deeply through your nose and slowly exhaling from your mouth. Breathe deeply for several minutes, because relaxation is very important before handling your Crystal.

2.

When you have relaxed, pick up your Crystal with your left hand and begin gazing upon it. Continue your rhythmic breathing. Now, say to yourself, *"Attune to the vibrations of*

Elestial Quartz. Merge my consciousness with the layers of this Crystal." Silently repeat these statements seven times, while you focus your concentration into the depth of the layers of your Crystal. Soon you will feel vibrations begin to rise within your body. When the vibrations begin, again repeat seven times, *"Attune to the vibrations of Elestial Quartz. Merge my consciousness with the layers of this Crystal." (At this point, your breathing will have become quite shallow.)*

Close your eyes now, and allow the visions to unfold. You may begin to experience sensations of lightheadedness, a drifting or floating sensation, as the vibrations of attunement to your Crystal grow stronger. Let yourself sink deeper and deeper into the Meditation. Impressions and pictures will begin to develop that address the dynamics of your consciousness, and the devices and reactionary behavior modes that the ego employs. At first the images may not be clearly visible, leaving only partial impressions to guide you toward understanding. In such cases, be patient, as subconscious understanding will have been achieved, reinforcing subsequent Meditations to be more productive on the conscious level.

3.

As your Meditation continues, you may experience Divine Light Vibrations that seem to pulse and/or grow stronger at some chakra centers than at others. Focus upon balancing your rate of vibration so that each chakra center is impacted upon equally. This can be accomplished by consciously predisposing yourself to opening each of your seven major chakra centers at the beginning of your Meditation, and will result in better identification of sites of imbalances, emotional wounds, developmental traumas and areas related to consciousness in need of transmutation. As you begin to visualize situations, interactions with people, moments of joy and sadness, impulses of greed and self-importance, moments of anger and doubt, you will begin to register those things about yourself that impede your growth toward realizing your true potential as an evolved, Light-minded being. You will reach an understanding of those aspects of your conscious being that need to be processed, resolved and transmuted. Elestial Quartz Meditation allows each soul incarnate the opportunity to come face to face with those aspects of him/herself that impede Light-minded behavior, and in as much as identifying a nonproductive and/or problematic situation is the first step toward resolving that situation, Elestial Quartz Crystals were given to mankind to be of service in assisting each soul incarnate in becoming The Divine Light Vibration that he or she was conceived to be.

4.

When you are ready to terminate your Elestial Quartz Crystal Meditation, slowly count backwards from ten to one. When you reach one, *REMAIN SEATED AND DO NOT OPEN YOUR EYES.* Now, visualize your body as the trunk of a towering oak tree, your arms as the branches and your legs as the roots. Watch as the roots pass from the bottoms of your feet, through the floor and anchor within the depths of Mother Earth. When you have completed this visualization, again count backwards from ten to one. At the count of one, open your eyes and breathe deeply several times, knowing that you are fully grounded in third dimension reality.

FIRE AGATE MEDITATION

Fire Agate combines the elements of Fire and Earth to produce systemic charging, balancing of energies and reinforcement of the chakra cord to facilitate stamina and Light-minded determination in the execution of one's Earthly responsibilities. Quite spectacular in appearance, Fire Agate's iridescent golds, reds, yellows, greens, blues and oranges awaken the senses, stimulating one's desire to maintain the enlightened path toward The Wisdom of One. By grounding etheric consciousness into the navel and base chakras, thereby establishing and/or strengthening the foundation and directive for service to Creation, Fire Agate offers mankind a high vibratory tool to counterbalance the debilitating effects of physical and mental stress resultant from processing third dimension realities.

Fire Agate can be found in Crystal and Jewelry Shops in cabochons, free-form polished chunks, rings, earrings and pendants. Price is dependent upon brilliance and the number of colors found shimmering within the brown base color of the Crystal. For purposes of Meditation, cabochons or free-form polished chunks are recommended *(and as it happens, are the least expensive form of Fire Agate)*.

1.

To prepare for your Fire Agate Meditation, select a Crystal that reflects an array of colors that strikes you both from intrinsic and intuitive standpoints. This will be a Crystal that literally "takes your breath away" as you gaze upon it. Cleanse and bless your Fire Agate in the prescribed manner before proceeding.

2.

To begin your Fire Agate Meditation, seat yourself in an upright position in a quiet, softly illuminated room. Begin to relax by initiating a rhythmic breathing sequence. Inhale deeply through the nose, hold the breath for three seconds and slowly exhale from the mouth. As you inhale, visualize cleansing Golden/White Light Vibrations entering your nose, traveling down your trachea, filling your lungs and heart center with glowing LoveLight Sensations. As you exhale, visualize tension and stress, hostility and resentment leaving your body in dark, cloudy swirls of energy. Bless yourself and your discordant energy in The Name of Yahweh, by The Spirit of Christ Jesus, as you cast these counterproductive energies unto the ether to find Peace.

3.

Pick up your Fire Agate in your left hand and begin to gaze upon it. Cradle your left hand in your right hand and allow both hands to rest in your lap. Hold the Fire Agate between the thumb and index finger of your left hand and begin to slowly tilt the Crystal back and forth to reveal the dazzling colors reflecting from deep within the Crystal. Repeat to yourself, *"Attune, Balance, Integrate, Ground."* Silently repeat these words again and again. Soon you may begin to experience warming or tingling sensations in your hands, arms and along your chakra cord. This is the attunement process taking place.

4.

Now, close your eyes and say to yourself, *"Attune to the Color Vibrations of Fire Agate."* Begin to visualize the brown ray of Fire Agate as a brown sphere encompassing your navel and base chakras. *(Spread the fingers of your right hand and place it between your navel and base chakras. This will help you in the placement of the brown sphere.)* Next, visualize the colors in your Fire Agate as swirling rays of Light above your head. Allow the swirling colors to enter your crown chakra and travel down the length of your chakra cord. Watch as the swirling colors meet and commingle with the color of the brown sphere. Watch as the brown sphere between your navel and base chakras begins to slowly rotate in a clockwise direction, revealing the iridescent color array seen in your Fire Agate. Feel the surges of energy along your chakra cord. Feel the Strength and Conviction filling you with Light-minded purpose. Feel your mind and body being balanced and revitalized by The Light of One.

5.

When you are ready to return from your Fire Agate Meditation, simply count backwards from ten to one. At the count of one, open your eyes and breathe deeply several times, inhaling through your nose and slowly exhaling from your mouth. Do not be in a hurry to move about; rather, allow yourself the time to savor the inspired, energized sensations that fill you.

FLUORITE MEDITATION

Fluorite, with its subtle color variations and striking shapes, makes it possible for mankind to access and comprehend Etheric Order, The Wisdom of Higher Organization, and integrate The Wisdom of Etheric Order into the conscious thought process. Impacting upon the 6th and 7th chakra areas, Fluorite's purples, blues, blue-greens, silvery-blues and golds amplify Divine Light Vibrations that assist in opening the crown chakra and third eye center, thereby allowing the free flow of Universal Truth into the conscious thought patterns of man. Once The Wisdom of Higher Consciousness has been accessed, mankind is better able to implement the precepts of Universal Law upon the Earth Plane. It is then that man's vision is no longer limited to the insights of a singular third dimension existence; rather, the interconnected life-function of all things born of Creation is seen and viewed with clarity.

Fluorite crystallizes in pyramidal, octahedral, sheet and cluster forms that graphically illustrate symmetrical and/or balanced relationships within and between individual and groups of Crystals. The balancing that Fluorite displays can be viewed as a sense of harmony that exists within the Crystal's growth function, and seems to portray a futuristic scene of how cities of Earth may evolve in structure. *(Indeed Native American cultures of the southwest built cliff and mountain cities that resembled the form of Fluorite Clusters.)*

1.

To prepare for your Fluorite Meditation, select a Fluorite specimen that appeals to your intuition and sense of color and shape. Fluorite can be purchased in its natural states as mentioned earlier or a cut and polished egg, sphere, obelisk or pyramid may be more to your liking. Whatever the case, select a Fluorite Meditation Partner that feels right for you. Cleanse and bless your Fluorite using The Sun and water, smudge or incense techniques.

2.

To begin your Meditation, situate yourself in a quiet room that is softly illuminated and adopt an upright seating position. Begin your rhythmic breathing sequence by inhaling through the nose and slowly exhaling from the mouth. As you inhale, visualize cleansing, radiant Golden/White Light Energy entering your nose, filling your lungs, chest cavity and heart center. As you exhale, visualize tension and anger, stress and frustration leaving your body in dark, cloudy swirls of discordant vibrations. Bless yourself and your discordant vibrations in The Name of Yahweh and cast these disruptive, counterproductive vibrations unto the ether to find Peaceful resolution. Continue your deep breathing for three to five minutes or until you feel that your body has become completely relaxed.

3.

Now, pick up your Fluorite Crystal in your left hand and begin to gaze upon it. With the index finger of your right hand, begin to stroke your Crystal and repeat to yourself, *"Attune to the vibrations of Fluorite. Attune. Attune. Attune to the vibrations of Fluorite."* Repeat these words several times. Then with your left hand, place your Fluorite Crystal against your third eye center. Now, slowly repeat these words to yourself, *"Attune, Balance, Integrate, Ground."* After a short time you may begin to experience energy movement in your third eye center and throughout your body. Again repeat the words, *"Attune, Balance, Integrate, Ground."* Continue your rhythmic breathing sequence and allow yourself to merge with the vibrations being amplified through your Fluorite Crystal.

After about ten minutes, you may begin to experience visionary sequences that depict ancient lands and cultures, or scenes that illustrate patterns of thought and behavior, or numerical references associated with statistical organization, or architectural structures that address application of Etheric Order to life upon the Earth Plane. Allow yourself to see The Wisdom of One as amplified through your Fluorite Crystal. Allow yourself to commune with and understand the integral nature of Harmony and balance that may come into existence upon the Earth. Allow yourself to see the future and hope for all things born of Creation.

4.

When you are ready to return to the reality of your Meditation room, simply count backwards from ten to one. When you reach one, open your eyes and *REMAIN SEATED.*

Do not stand up immediately. Breathe deeply, inhaling through the nose and slowly exhaling from the mouth several times. Remain seated for five minutes to allow yourself time to process the information that you have received. It might be suggested that a log be kept of the visionary sequences that you experience during your Fluorite Meditations, as there can be a recurring theme designed to transmit specific information to you. Then you will develop a deeper understanding of the nature of Etheric Order, as well as comprehend your role in this life upon Mother Earth.

KUNZITE MEDITATION

The development and merging of third eye clarity with the motivation of the heart center is the blessing bestowed by Kunzite; that is, by attuning to the lavender/pink ray amplified through Kunzite, mankind is able to clearly perceive the Light-minded motivations of Love for all things, thereby giving birth to Compassion. Kunzite aids in awakening the dormant understanding that mankind is truly integrally related to all the life born of Creation. Kunzite facilitates mankind's development of tenderness and gentle concern in our actions toward and interactions with our brethren in the various Kingdoms upon Mother Earth.

The lavender/pink ray amplified through Kunzite provides a soothing, comforting sensation for the entire energy complex of the human body, and assists in the release and/or transformation of discordant energy systems attached to or surrounding the body. Kunzite is the Crystalline form whose purpose is to aid mankind in overcoming shortsighted, egocentric behaviors that impede the expression of Love, Mercy and Compassion. And as a gentle messenger of The Light, Kunzite offers itself as a tool to assist mankind in making the transition from self-serving, aggressive behavior modes to the gentle, altruistic concern for and communion with all things born of Creation.

Kunzite Crystals can be found in a variety of colors. From clear transparencies to lime green and from gentle lavender/pink to a rich red/violet, Kunzite can amplify a wide range of Divine Light Vibrations. But for the purpose of this Meditation, let us maintain focus upon only the lavender/pink variety. Although Kunzite Crystals do command a fairly high premium, the benefits derived from these gentle yet dynamic members of the Quartz Family well warrant the expense.

1.

To prepare for your Kunzite Meditation, select a Kunzite Crystal *(a natural, terminated specimen is best)* whose color intensity is subtle, not overwhelming, but displays a discernable, gentle blend of pink and lavender. Cleanse and bless your Crystal by washing it in cool, running water and placing it in sunlight for an afternoon, or by smudging the Crystal, or by using Tingshaw. Cleansing and blessing your Kunzite Crystal can most effectively be done by combining any two or three cleansing procedures with a prayer designed to invoke Divine Light Vibrations in The Name of Yahweh.

2.

Situate yourself in an upright position with your feet flat on the floor in a quiet, softly illuminated room. Begin your rhythmic breathing sequence by inhaling through the nose and exhaling from the mouth. As you inhale, visualize Golden/White Light Vibrations entering your nose, filling your lungs and heart center with cleansing, glowing Golden/White Light Vibrations. As you exhale, visualize tensions, anxieties, frustrations and angers leaving your body in dark, cloudy swirls of energy. Bless your discordant vibrations in The Name of

Yahweh, as you cast these vibrations unto the ether to find Peace.

3.

Pick up your Kunzite Crystal with your left hand and begin to gaze upon it. Observe the color of your Crystal, noticing areas that are predominantly pink and other areas that are predominantly lavender. Observe the delicate beauty of the areas of your Kunzite Crystal where the lavender and pink merge as one soft, benevolent color. Focus your attention upon the area where the lavender and pink unite. See the gentle union of lavender and pink and say to yourself, *"Attune, Balance, Integrate, Ground."* Repeat these words several times. Now, place the index finger of your right hand upon your Kunzite Crystal and stroke it tenderly. Say to yourself, *"Attune to the lavender/pink ray of Kunzite. Attune. Attune. Attune to the lavender/pink ray of Kunzite."* Repeat these statements several times. After a time, you may begin to experience tingling or warming sensations in your hands, fingers and arms. You may also experience surges of energy at your third eye and heart chakras.

4.

Now, visualize the lavender/pink ray of Kunzite glowing, radiating at both your third eye and heart centers. See the lavender/pink ray of Kunzite filling and gently energizing your third eye and heart chakras. Now, as you inhale, visualize a pink beam of Divine Light Energy traveling up from your heart center and connecting with your third eye. As you exhale, visualize a lavender beam of Divine Light Energy traveling down from your third eye center and connecting with your heart chakra. Hold this visualization for ten to fifteen minutes.

Now, visualize the lavender/pink ray glowing at each of your chakras beginning with your third eye and moving down to your base chakra. See the lavender/pink ray of Kunzite radiating its warmth, its soothing comfort throughout your chakra system. Now, visualize the lavender/pink ray spreading from your chakras and filling your entire body with sensations of compassionate warmth and tenderness. Feel the blissful caress and enchantment bestowed upon you by the lavender/pink ray of Kunzite. Now, visualize the lavender/pink ray spreading from your body to encompass everything within your Meditation room. See all of your surroundings colored with the lavender/pink ray. Everything around you, your chair, the curtains, your plants, the carpet, the table, the books and bookcase - everything around you now glows with the gentle radiance of Kunzite's lavender/pink ray. Hold this visualization for up to fifteen minutes.

5.

When you are ready to return to the reality of your Meditation room, simply count backwards from ten to one. When you reach one, open your eyes. Remain seated. Breathe deeply several times, inhaling through the nose and exhaling from the mouth. Remain seated. Allow yourself adequate time to fully integrate into third dimension reality before you attempt to leave your seated position. And by all means, savor the Tranquil Conscience that has settled upon you, filling you with renewed vigor to implement Patience, Mercy, Love and Compassion for all things born of Creation.

KYANITE MEDITATION

with Selenite, Tabular Quartz, Azurite and Rose Quartz Crystals

Kyanite is benevolently transformational in activity, impacting upon and aiding the throat *(5th)* chakra in the transmutation of debilitating fears and anxieties. When in use, the blue and white patterns of Kyanite are known to change in color intensity. Kyanite can lose most if not all of its white markings, becoming crystallized and evolving into a rich azure blue throughout. As the vibrations amplified through this stone are assimilated by the throat chakra, the azure blue color intensifies.

Many times, when fears of rejection, feelings of inadequacy in interpersonal relationships and questions of intellectual validity and self-worth arise, the throat chakra can be identified as the site of restriction and/or closure. The closing of the throat chakra is evidenced by occasions of anxiety, stuttering, hot flashes and the inability or unwillingness to communicate verbally for fear of being exposed or discovered to be somehow lacking in competence or worthiness. Often when verbal dysfunctions arise in people who ordinarily are quite articulate, the verbal dysfunction can be directly attributed to submerged fears located at the throat chakra. By attuning to the gentle blue ray amplified through Kyanite, submerged fears can be identified and transmuted, restoring confidence in one's ability to communicate effectively.

1.

Additional Crystals and Minerals are required for this Meditation: a Clear Quartz Tabular Crystal, a Selenite Rosette, a Rose Quartz Crystal and an Azurite Nodule, or an Azurite/Malachite cabochon. Prepare these Minerals for your Meditation by using the appropriate cleansing and blessing procedure. The first portion of this Meditation can be performed either in a seated or reclined position. Hold the Selenite Rosette in your left hand and the Tabular Crystal in your right hand. Breathe deeply, inhaling through the nose and slowly exhaling from the mouth. Relax and allow yourself to attune to the vibrations of the Selenite and Tabular Crystal. Now, while holding the Selenite and Tabular Crystal, touch the index finger and thumb of your right hand against the index finger and thumb of your left hand. Maintain this contact position and continue your deep breathing. Consciously say to yourself, *"Attune to the vibrations of Selenite and Tabular Quartz."* Slowly repeat this statement several times and continue your deep breathing. Relax and soon you will feel the energy vibrations beginning to rise in you.

2.

Now, pick up the Azurite and hold it against your throat chakra with the index fingers of both hands, while resting both thumbs on your chest just below the clavical. Hold the Azurite in place for no more than one to three minutes per Meditation. *(Prolonged placement of Azurite Nodules upon any part of the body can surface submerged thought and behavior patterns that may require considerable time to process. It is therefore recommended that only short periods of exposure to Azurite Nodules be given, or that Azurite/Malachite cabochons be used to soften the impact of Azurite.)* Now, close your eyes and say to yourself, *"Azurite, penetrate through my fears, and bring to the surface the reality of the fears that entrap me. Attune to the vibrations of Azurite. Attune. Attune. Attune to the vibrations of Azurite."* Repeat these statements three times. Soon you will feel a growing intensity in the vibrations at your throat chakra. You may well experience sequences of visions that depict situations exemplifying the fears lodged at your throat chakra.

3.

Now, put aside the Tabular Crystal, Selenite Rosette and Azurite. Seat yourself in an upright position and breathe deeply several times. Pick up your Kyanite with your left hand and place it directly against your throat chakra. Say to yourself, *"Attune to the vibrations of Kyanite. Attune. Attune. Attune to the blue ray of Kyanite."* Slowly repeat these statements several times until you begin to feel energy movement at your throat chakra. Now, relax and hold the Kyanite in place for ten minutes.

4.

Remove the Kyanite from your throat chakra and close it in the palm of your left hand. Pick up your Rose Quartz with your right hand and hold it in place against your throat chakra. Now, say to yourself, *"Attune to the benevolent pink ray of Rose Quartz. Attune. Attune. Attune to the pink ray of Rose Quartz."* Slowly repeat these statements again and again and relax. Soon you will feel the warm, gentle glow of Rose Quartz caressing your throat chakra, aiding in the facilitation and transformation of any emotional wounds. Hold the Rose Quartz in place for five to fifteen minutes to allow the pink ray to be fully assimilated by your throat chakra.

5.

Remove the Rose Quartz from your throat chakra and put it aside. Open your left hand *(that has probably been pulsating while you were holding the Rose Quartz against your throat chakra with your right hand)* and gaze upon your Kyanite. Place your right index finger upon the Kyanite and visualize the color of your stone at your throat chakra, aiding in the transmutation of surfaced fears, doubts and anxieties. Hold the visualization for three minutes or for as long as you can.

6.

Carry your Kyanite in your pocket or purse so that the energy vibration of your stone is constantly near you for the next seven days . Also, during this period you should practice visualizing the blue ray of Kyanite at your throat chakra. And at night, place your Kyanite on your dresser or next to your bed so that you can gaze upon it just before retiring. You will notice that over the seven day period that your Kyanite will have become progressively more blue, in fact crystallizing as you attune to and absorb your stone's transformational energy. *(Frequently, after the first few minutes that the stone is attuned to, Kyanite shows a noticeable change in color intensity.)*

LAPIS LAZULI MEDITATION

Lapis Lazuli has been revered as a stone of transformation and Higher Consciousness for thousands of years, and the application of Lapis Lazuli to mankind's evolving consciousness is as pertinent today as it was eons ago. The ancients utilized Lapis to bridge mortal consciousness with The Will of the Universe, for the deep blue of Lapis represents the midnight sky and the golden Pyrite flecks that abound in higher grades of Lapis symbolize the stars and constellations. By attuning to the vibrations amplified through Lapis, especially during rituals and initiation ceremonies, the ancients learned to merge the consciousness of man with The Consciousness of God. This ritual and practical use of Lapis helped early man to discern the elements of Universal Law and to comprehend the dynamics of Universal Life. Lapis offered the ancients a clear picture of Universal Form, thereby enabling the user to tap into the Wisdom that connects the soul to The Infinite Body of God.

For many, Lapis Lazuli holds the key to unlocking dormant channeling and visionary abilities, as this stone can elevate third eye consciousness to enable the user to access intergalactic communication modes. This is to say that Lapis can facilitate the expression of the intuitive voice, as well as aid in the reception of information transmitted by Ascended Teachers, Spirit Guides and other messengers of The Infinite One.

As a tool of facilitation, one of the most beneficial characteristics of Lapis Lazuli is its ability to assist in the release of emotional stress that leads to muscular tension and stiffness, especially muscular tension in the upper body about the head, neck and shoulders. This characteristic of Lapis addresses mankind's often debilitating habit of inflicting punishment and guilt upon one's self for some behavior deficiency (the *"if only I had"* syndrome). By placing Lapis directly upon the neck and shoulder areas where much emotional tension can develop, the user can untangle the knots of emotional dysfunction and learn to forgive him/herself for counterproductive thoughts and behaviors. *(As noted in other parts of this text, success derived from utilizing the vibrations amplified through Quartz/Mineral specimens is dependent upon the users' commitment, diligence and readiness to attune to the energies offered by the Quartz/Mineral Kingdom, as well as willingness to acknowledge and resolve personal conflicts.)*

Though Lapis Lazuli is mined in South America, the highest grades of Lapis are exported from Afghanistan. Lapis rings, pendants, cabochons, polished eggs, spheres, obelisks, pyramids and tumbled stones are readily available in Crystal Shops and Metaphysical Stores. *(Note: In purchasing Lapis jewelry, it is suggested that the setting is left open in the back so that the stone is allowed to make contact with the skin. This assists in the attunement process, as it affords a purer vibration of the stone to enter the auric body.)* For Meditation purposes, select a Lapis specimen that appeals to you both intuitively and from the standpoint of the stone's inherent beauty.

1.

To begin your Meditation, seat yourself in an upright position in a quiet, dimly lit room. Inhale deeply through the nose and slowly exhale from the mouth. As you inhale, visualize

Golden/White Light Energy entering your body through your nose, filling your lungs, chest cavity and heart center with warm, glowing, comforting sensations. As you exhale, visualize frustration and tension leaving your body through your mouth in dark, cloudy, swirling energy vibrations. Bless yourself in The Name of Yahweh, as you release your discordant vibrations unto the ether to find Peace.

2.

Now, pick up your specimen of Lapis Lazuli *(that has been cleansed and blessed)* in your left hand and begin to gaze upon the Crystal. Say to yourself, *"Attune to the vibrations of Lapis. Attune. Attune. Attune to the vibrations of Lapis."* Repeat these statements several times until you begin to feel yourself merging with the stone. Then say, *"In The Name of Yahweh, allow my consciousness to merge with The Will of The Infinite One."* Repeat this statement three times. At this point, your breathing will have become shallow and you may notice energy movement within your chakra system.

3.

Now, close your eyes and visualize the color and markings of your Lapis specimen at your third eye center. When you are able to see the color and markings of your Lapis at your third eye center, slowly raise the stone in your left hand and place it over your third eye center. Relax, as your journey into the Ethereal Plane will have begun. Embrace the physical, visual and intuitive sensations that you encounter. Allow yourself to experience The Divine Light Vibrations of Absolute Truth. Allow The Wisdom of the Universe to flow through every fiber of your being. Allow yourself to merge with The Conscience of One.

4.

When you are ready to return to the reality of your Meditation setting, slowly count backwards from ten to one. When you reach one, open your eyes. Remain seated. Take a few deep breaths, stretch your arms and shoulders upward, opening and closing your hands into fists, and remain seated for three to five minutes. Do not be in a hurry to move around in your Meditation room. It is most probable that after completing this Meditation sequence you will simply wish to remain quiet so that you may reflect upon your experience. Performing this Meditation over a period of time will allow you to experience a variety of altered states of consciousness, and you will perceive and assimilate knowledge that will enhance every aspect of mortal existence. Cherish your Lapis Lazuli Meditation Partner, as with it you may learn to embrace the very Heart of God.

MALACHITE MEDITATION

Malachite is one of the oldest and most versatile Minerals used for amplifying the green ray of The Divine Light Spectrum. A Copper-related Mineral with swirls, blotches and rings of various shades of green and blue-green, Malachite has been revered and imbued with a wide variety of Spiritual and Mystical Properties by Shaman and the Priest/Keepers of metaphysical and esoteric doctrines from several different cultures. Historically, Malachite has been thought to bestow a blessing of protection upon travelers who undertake arduous journeys, as well as a protective energy presence for warriors going into battle. Malachite has also been a Mineral associated with royalty, a stone thought to ward off discordant energies and a tool for divining and forecasting future events.

However, in our practice of Healing Facilitation and Crystal Meditation, we utilize the green ray amplified through Malachite to assist mortal consciousness in surfacing the energy and memory of submerged emotional traumas associated with learning The Lessons of Existence. When placed at the navel, solar plexus or heart chakras (and in the case of Malachite/Azurite placement at the third eye chakra), Malachite can assist mortal consciousness in accessing and accepting the true motivation and reality of painful emotional experiences that can impede the evolution of God-Conscious Being. Additionally,

Malachite can assist in transmuting problematic emotional energies, while simultaneously facilitating the understanding of life-sequences and stimulating conscious well-being. (Note: It is recommended that soul incarnates who are very sensitive to emotional issues use Rose Quartz in conjunction with Malachite to help soften the activity and effects that Malachite can product.)

Though mined in many parts of the world, the most abundant deposits of Malachite have been found in Zaire. Much of the Malachite mined in Zaire is shipped to other third world countries for processing into animal and fetish carvings, geometric shapes, boxes, pendants and cabochon forms. Readily available from novelty shops, jewelers, New Age and Rock & Mineral Shops, Malachite can easily be found in the size, shape and price range to accommodate all who wish to commune with the benevolent, transformational energy that Malachite so willingly offers to facilitate the evolutionary journey of man.

1.

To prepare for your Malachite Meditation, select a Malachite specimen that seems to "call out to you", as if the Malachite specimen were asking you to pick it up. In selecting the appropriate specimen, be aware that Malachite specimens that show a bull's-eye pattern can quickly penetrate layers of consciousness to reveal suppressed emotional traumas. Also, the more striking and diverse the color contrast of the bull's-eye, the more efficient (and in some cases, the more ruthless) is the Malachite specimen in helping to surface the energy and memory of submerged emotional traumas from this as well as past lifetimes.

2.

Cleanse and bless your Malachite specimen in the prescribed manner, washing it and placing it in sunlight for an afternoon, prior to positioning yourself for Meditation. It is suggested that sea salts not be used for cleansing Crystals and Minerals and especially not for cleansing Malachite. Not only do sea salts alter the natural resonance range of Crystals and Minerals, but in the case of Malachite and other "soft" Minerals, sea salts will stimulate decomposition of the Mineral.

3.

Select a quiet, dimly lit room for your Malachite Meditation, and seat yourself in an upright position. Initiate a rhythmic breathing sequence by inhaling deeply through the nose, holding the breath for three seconds, then slowly exhaling from the mouth. As you inhale, visualize cleansing, Golden/White Light Energy entering your nose, traveling down your trachea and filling your lungs and heart center with glowing, radiant LoveLight Sensations. As you exhale, visualize tension, anxiety, confusion, fear and uncertainty leaving your body in dark, cloudy swirls of energy that you expel from your mouth. Bless these and all other discordant vibrations associated with your consciousness, as you cast them unto the ether, in The Name of Yahweh, to find Peace. Allow yourself to relax, free of stress and counterproductive energies. Allow self to relax.

4.

Now, pick up your Malachite with your left hand and begin to gaze upon it. Study the color patterns and the movement of the swirls, blotches and bands of the different shades of green in your Malachite. Gently stroke your Malachite with the index finger of your right hand, and silently repeat these words several times, *"Attune, Balance, Integrate, Ground"*. Allow self to bond with the green ray amplified through your Malachite specimen.

Now, close your eyes and visualize the pattern of the green ray of your Malachite filling your navel chakra with warm, transformational energies. Feel your navel chakra begin to open wider and wider to accept more and more of the green ray of Malachite. Now, visualize both your navel and solar plexus chakras pulsing with the green ray of Malachite. Again, silently repeat these words several times, *"Attune, Balance, Integrate, Ground"*. Now, visualize your navel, solar plexus and heart chakras each pulsing and expanding as they are filled by the green ray of Malachite. Once again, silently repeat the words, *"Attune, Balance, Integrate, Ground"*, several times. Allow self to feel the inspired Divine Light Vibrations of Malachite at work assisting you to access suppressed memories of emotional trauma. Allow self to embrace the pain of yesterday with Forgiveness and Love, thereby releasing self from judgements, reactions, fears and anxieties. Feel the green ray of Malachite as it warms you and fills you with the courage and willingness to engage all life-conditions with the purpose of understanding and resolving the pain, suffering, fear and uncertainty from the Karmic past. Allow self to embrace the green ray of Malachite and allow self to be free.

5.

When you are ready to return from your Malachite Meditation, simply count backwards from ten to one. At the count of one, open your eyes, breathe deeply and remain seated. Reflect upon your Meditation and allow self to comprehend the reality of emotional release and Karmic Resolution. Remain seated. Breathe deeply and allow self to slowly reintegrate into the third dimension reality of your Meditation room. Breathe deeply and allow yesterday's pain and sorrow to know Forgiveness in The Light of One. Breathe deeply and allow self to simply "be".

METEORITE MEDITATION

Meteorites are usually metallic-based stones that are the remnants of galactic bodies that fall to Earth. Found in numerous locations around the world, Meteorites have long been used as objects of worship and as tools of ritual and evocation. Meteorites fashioned into or incorporated in spiritual implements are believed to be endowed with special spiritual powers by virtue of the Meteorite's origin and the unique manner in which they appear on Earth.

In Meditation, Meteorites can unlock memories of ancient incarnations on distant planets. Accepting and understanding past galactic incarnations can facilitate one's comprehension of his/her true mental/physical/emotional evolution. Meteorites can also awaken man's conscious knowledge of contact with alternate life-forms and/or extraterrestrial beings during this incarnation. For many, attunement to the energies amplified through Meteorites can be almost instantaneous, as information about interplanetary life and extraterrestrials may have already been revealed to many in dreams, through channel or in visionary sequences.

Meteorites can be purchased from New Age and Rock Shops, as well as from private collectors who advertise in Gem and

Mineral magazines. Small metallic-based Meteorites *(1-5 gram weight)* can be acquired inexpensively, but the heavier stones may be priced at over $1,000. Tektites, which are glassy Meteorites that are green to black in color, command higher prices than do their metallic counterparts. Both types of Meteorites make excellent Meditation Partners. Allow your intuition to guide you in your selection of Meteorite type and color.

1.

To prepare for your Meteorite Meditation, select a Meteorite that feels "good and right" when held in the palm of your hand. Do not be surprised if you feel a bit lightheaded shortly after picking up the stone. *(Some report an immediate "ringing in the ears" sensation, but this is neither harmful, nor uncommon.)* Cleanse and bless your Meteorite in advance in the prescribed manner. It is further suggested that you store your Meteorite in a place where it will receive an abundance of sunshine daily.

2.

Begin your Meteorite Meditation by seating yourself in an upright position in a softly illuminated, quiet room. Initiate your rhythmic breathing sequence by deeply inhaling through the nose, holding the breath for three seconds and slowly exhaling from the mouth. As you inhale, visualize cleansing Golden/White Light Energy entering your nose, traveling down your trachea, filling your lungs and heart center with glowing LoveLight Sensations. As you exhale, visualize tension and stress leaving your body in dark, cloudy swirls of discordant energy. Bless yourself and your discordant energy in The Name of Yahweh, by The Spirit of Christ Jesus, as you cast this dissonant, counterproductive energy unto the ether to find Peace.

3.

Now, pick up your Meteorite in your left hand and begin to gaze upon it. Realize that you hold a stone that originated far beyond the limits of Earth and that your Meteorite may have traveled millions of miles through dozens of galactic systems before arriving on Planet Earth. Realize that the energies amplified through your Meteorite are designed to awaken your memories of some of the places your Meteorite has been. Allow yourself to merge with the energies amplified through your Meteorite by closing your eyes and repeating to yourself, *"Attune, Balance, Integrate, Ground."* Repeat these words several times. Place the index finger of your right hand upon your Meteorite and repeat to yourself, *"In The Name of Yahweh, let me attune to the energy of this Meteorite. Let me see the mystery unfold. In The Name of Yahweh, by The Spirit of Christ Jesus, let the mystery unfold - let me see the distant planets and other beings of the Universe."*

4.

You will begin to notice a sense of lightness about your physical body. Shortly thereafter, you will experience a separation from your reality of Earth and begin to travel to other planetary systems. Allow yourself to drift and float through galactic memories. *(At this time, it is not uncommon to register strong energy surges along your chakra cord.)* You may experience images, faint representations, of places and creatures that you can not fully identify. Do not be overly concerned with identifying what you see. Rather, disengage your conscious mind and allow yourself to experience the sensations and images that commune with you. You will come to understand the meaning of what you have experienced in due course. Allow yourself to experience the wonders of the Universe.

5.

When you are ready to return from your Meteorite Meditation, count backwards from ten to one. At the count of one, *DO NOT OPEN YOUR EYES AND REMAIN SEATED.* Now, visualize your body as the trunk of a majestic oak tree. From the bottoms of your feet, visualize the roots of the tree as they penetrate through the floor and sink deeply into the bosom of Mother Earth, anchoring, grounding your very existence in third dimension. Again count backwards from ten to one. At the count of one, open your eyes and breathe deeply several times. Do not be in a hurry to move about. Instead, sit quietly and reflect upon your Meditation. *(It is recommended that you have a pen and pad handy to record your experiences immediately following your Meditation. This will help you to compare future Meditations and results.)*

MOONSTONE MEDITATION
with Amethyst and Rose Quartz

Moonstones exhibit shimmering, opalescent colors in shades of blue, pink, red, gray, orange, salmon, peach, lavender and white that work through the heart center to assist in balancing emotionally charged circumstances. As a gentle messenger of Divine Light, Moonstones present themselves as tools for mankind's use in establishing and maintaining Harmony during times of emotional upheaval and during times of physiological imbalances that result in the expression of anxiety, frustration, anger, projection and resentment. Moonstones can be used in Meditation by themselves, but when combined with Amethyst at the third eye and Rose Quartz at the heart chakra, Moonstones work in tandem with Rose Quartz and Amethyst to effectively aid in transmuting imbalanced emotional states.

1.

To prepare for your Moonstone Meditation, select three tumbled or polished Moonstone cabochons of different color varieties that intuitively and aesthetically appeal to you. Also select an Amethyst and a Rose Quartz Crystal for use in this Meditation. After cleansing and blessing your Crystals, hold your Moonstones in your left hand and begin gazing upon them, drinking in the shimmering, translucent colors.

2.

Situate yourself in a quiet, softly illuminated room in an upright position. Begin your breathing sequence by inhaling deeply through the nose and slowly exhaling from the mouth. As you inhale, visualize cleansing Golden/White Light Vibrations entering your nose, filling your lungs and heart center. As you exhale, visualize anxiety, tension, frustration and stress leaving your body in dark, cloudy swirls of energy. Bless your discordant vibrations in The Name of Yahweh, as you cast your discordant energies unto the ether to find Peace.

3.

Now, assume a comfortable position on the floor, lying on your back, arms at your sides, legs uncrossed and lying flat in front of you. With your right hand, place your Rose Quartz at your heart center, then with your three Moonstones make a triangular pattern *(pointing toward your chin)* around your Rose Quartz. *(All Crystals will have been cleansed and blessed in advance.)* Place your right hand over the Crystals at your heart chakra for the duration of this Meditation. Now, with your left hand, place place the Amethyst Crystal over your third eye and hold it in place.

4.

Close your eyes and breathe deeply several times. Now, say to yourself, *"Attune to the vibrations of Amethyst, Rose Quartz and Moonstone. Attune, Balance, Integrate, Ground."* Repeat these statements several times, then allow the infusion process to commence.

As you hold the Amethyst, Rose Quartz and Moonstone against your body, you may experience sensations of energy movement between your third eye and heart center. You may experience energy surges, throbbing sensations in your hands and fingers and tingling or warming sensations in your arms and along your spinal column. These physical sensations are frequently experienced in varying degrees of intensity, but more common is the relaxed, composed, Tranquil state that results from balancing and transmuting discordant emotional states.

5.

As you hold the Crystals against your body, visualize the circumstances, people, places and other elements that comprise your emotionally charged situations. Relax and allow the visualization to unfold. Now, say to yourself, *"Amethyst, let me clearly see the underlying reasons for my emotional distress."* Relax. After one minute, say to yourself, *"Moonstones, assist me in balancing my emotional dilemma."* Relax for another minute, then say to yourself, *"Rose Quartz, aid me in resolving the emotional wounds of my heart center."*

Lie still and quiet, allowing yourself to be enveloped by the energy transmitted through your Crystals. Lie still and observe the subtle shift in your perceptions about your emotionally charged situations. Sense the release of inappropriate emotional energy. Feel the Tranquility filling you, as you consciously balance the energies of your emotional being.

6.

When you are ready to return to the reality of your Meditation setting, simply count backwards from ten to one.

When you reach one, open your eyes, but remain in your position on the floor. Do not be in a hurry to stand up and move around. Remain on the floor for one to three minutes and take several deep breaths before sitting up. Remain seated on the floor until you feel fully integrated within third dimension reality.

Your Moonstone Meditation will have revealed a number of pertinent issues designed to enable you to better manage your emotional energies. Take the insights and Harmony offered by Amethyst, Rose Quartz and Moonstones and allow yourself to be free of emotional bondage and counterproductive *(reactionary)* behavior patterns. Allow yourself the opportunity to simply "be".

OBSIDIAN MEDITATION

Formed as the result of volcanic flows that dried very quickly, Obsidian has been used to fashion spear points, arrowheads and cutting tools since prehistoric times, and has also been valued for its high spiritual vibration. Black Obsidian displays many faces *(or forms)* that show mankind the presence of The Light within darkness. Used by Alchemists, Shamans, Spiritualists and Light-workers to aid in repelling discordant vibrations, Obsidian can amplify and transmit an extremely high frequency of Divine Light Energy by directing crown chakra Light Energy transmissions into the base chakra to conscionably assist in the direction and maintenance of survival drives. However, Obsidian goes beyond simply facilitating basal directives, as its purpose is indeed to illustrate to mankind that within the darkness of defeat, despair and depression, The Light of Higher Consciousness and hope awaits discovery.

One of the most profound Obsidian experiences can occur by gazing upon and Meditating with Rainbow Obsidian. Going far beyond the impact and influence of its relatives, Gold and Silver Sheen Obsidian, Rainbow Obsidian can display an amazing, breathtaking array of greens, reds, blues, golds, lavenders, purples and silver that serve to integrate elements of Ethereal Consciousness into the base chakra function, thereby tempering and/or aiding in the transmutation of the survival and ego-identification drives of the base chakra with The Consciousness of Divine Will. Rainbow Obsidian is indeed one of the most significant tools offered for mankind's evolving enlightenment, and most dramatically illustrates to man that within the darkest depths of night every color of the rainbow vibrates with purpose and Love.

Snowflake Obsidian and Apache Tears are two popular varieties of Obsidian, and Gold and Silver Obsidian are also important tools of conscience. Snowflake Obsidian dramatizes the birth and coexistence of Golden/White Light Vibrations within the solid, black protection of Obsidian. The transparency of Apache Tears illustrates that The Light, which is The Truth of all things, passes unfettered through the veil of darkness and illusion. Both stones are good for psychic protection, but Apache Tears are commonly thought to be more efficient in this area. Gold and Silver Sheen Obsidian are two very dramatic grounding agents that direct crown chakra energy into the base chakra for the purpose of facilitating The Consciousness of One in mankind's daily activities. And Mahogany Obsidian with its brown and black honeycomb appearance integrates navel and base chakra functions to assist in achieving stamina, stimulating cooperation and maintaining focus upon Earthly tasks.

Obsidian Crystals are readily available in a variety of forms. Gift shops, jewelers and Crystal shops offer tumbled, polished eggs, spheres, pyramids, obelisks, pendants, necklaces, earrings and natural slabs of Obsidian. Fortunately, most varieties of Obsidian are affordable, but the larger sizes of Sheen and Rainbow Obsidian can be costly.

1.

To prepare for your Obsidian Meditation, select a variety of Obsidian Crystal that intuitively draws your attention and is pleasing to your senses. The shape of the Obsidian Crystal that you choose is also a matter of personal preference, but spheres and eggs seem to be the most popular Meditation shapes. After cleansing and blessing your Crystal, you are ready to begin your Meditation.

2.

Begin your Meditation by situating yourself in an upright position with both feet flat on the floor in a quiet, softly illuminated room. Initiate your rhythmic breathing sequence by inhaling through your nose and exhaling from your mouth. *(It is suggested that The LoveLight Prayer/Invocation, The 23rd Psalm and Affirmations are performed prior to engaging in Obsidian Meditation.)* As you inhale, visualize cleansing Golden/White Light Vibrations entering your nose, filling your lungs, chest cavity and heart center with warm, Loving sensations. As you exhale, visualize tension, stress, frustration, resentment, anxiety and anger leaving your body in dark, cloudy swirls of discordant energy. Bless your discordant vibrations in The Name of Yahweh and cast them unto the ether to find Peaceful resolution.

3.

Now, pick up your Obsidian Crystal in your left hand and begin to gaze upon it. Notice the depth of color, the rich, satiny luster of your black Crystal. Observe the additional colors that live within the midnight mood of your Obsidian Crystal. Now, say to yourself, *"Attune, Balance, Integrate, Ground."* Repeat these words three times. Then place the index finger of your right hand upon your Obsidian Crystal and begin to stroke it gently. Now, say to yourself, *"Attune to the depths of Obsidian. Attune. Attune. Attune to the depths of the black ray of Obsidian."*

After a time, you may experience tingling, warmth or chilling sensations along the length of your spinal column, from your crown to your base chakra, down your legs and into your feet. This effect is your energy system attuning to The Divine Light Vibrations amplified through your Obsidian Crystal and should not cause alarm. Relax and allow yourself to merge with and absorb the energies being transmitted by your Obsidian Crystal.

4.

Now, visually fix the black color of Obsidian at your base chakra. See your base chakra as a liquid pool of Black Obsidian, pulsating with black Light Vibrations that ground you through your base chakra to the very consciousness of Earthly existence. In the case of colored Obsidians *(Rainbow, Gold and Silver Sheen, Mahogany and Snowflake)* also visualize the shimmering colors within your Obsidian as swirling Divine Light Vibrations above your head. Now, watch as the swirling Divine Light Vibrations above your head penetrate your crown chakra, slowly travel the length of your chakra cord and splash into the liquid pool of Black Obsidian at your base chakra. Watch as the shimmering colors commingle with the Black Obsidian, integrating etheric constructs of Divine Order with the dynamics of Earthly survival modes.

Hold this visualization for up to ten minutes. Allow your Obsidian Crystal to illuminate those aspects of your Earthly reality that have been hidden away from view. Allow The Light of Truth to illuminate the chambers where delusion, self-importance and the compulsions for material acquisition lie veiled by ego-facilitating, conditioned devices and attitudes. Allow your Obsidian Crystal to assist you to clearly see the reality of your thought and behavior patterns as pertains to your survival upon Planet Earth. Allow The Light of Truth to penetrate and illuminate the depths of darkness, and know that all things of Love and Conscience exist within the spectrum of Divine Light Vibration. And know too that indeed The Light and darkness exist as One.

5.

To terminate your Obsidian Meditation, slowly count backwards from ten to one. At the count of one, open your eyes and breathe deeply several times. Remain seated until you feel fully integrated, and reflect upon your Meditation experience.

ORTHOCLASE MEDITATION

Orthoclase is a Potassium Aluminum Silicate that, when attuned to, gently escorts its user into the deepest states of Meditation. Facilitating the expression of an open, evolved heart chakra during the Meditation process, Orthoclase initiates sensations of comfort, calm and security that impress upon the conscious mind the need and value of living upon Mother Earth with dynamics of enlightened heart chakra functions directing every thought, act and behavior tendency. Orthoclase helps the seeker of enlightenment to experience evolved states of consciousness that make it possible for a greater cooperative effort between the conscious mind and the intuitive self to develop. This allows and encourages the acknowledgement of the intuitive voice as a viable and necessary source of information. By accepting Orthoclase as a benevolent guide into the heart-centered reality of The Wisdom of One, mankind can learn to move through Karmic Resolution and effect Soul Evolution, thereby completing the ascension toward the moment of Harvest.

1.

To prepare for your Orthoclase Meditation, select an Orthoclase cluster that can be comfortably held in the palm of your hand. Natural, terminated clusters of Orthoclase are recommended for this Meditation and can be purchased from most New Age or Rock & Mineral Shops. Cleanse and bless your Orthoclase in the prescribed manner prior to your Meditation.

2.

To begin your Orthoclase Meditation, seat yourself in an upright position in a quiet, softly illuminated room. Initiate your rhythmic breathing sequence by inhaling deeply through your nose, holding the breath for three seconds and slowly exhaling from your mouth. As you inhale, visualize cleansing Golden/White Light Vibrations entering your nose, traveling down your trachea, filling your chest and heart chakra with glowing LoveLight Sensations. As you exhale, visualize dark, cloudy swirls of discordant energy leaving your body. Bless yourself and feelings of frustration, resentment, hostility, fear and anger in The Name of Yahweh, by The Spirit of Christ Jesus, as you cast these counterproductive, inflammatory vibrations unto the ether to find Peace.

3.

Pick up your Orthoclase cluster in your left hand and begin to gaze upon it. After a short time, place the index finger of your right hand upon the Orthoclase and gently stroke the cluster. As you stroke the cluster, repeat to yourself, *"Attune, Balance, Integrate, Ground."* Slowly repeat these words to yourself several times.

Now, close your eyes and repeat to yourself, *"Attune to the vibrations of Orthoclase. In The Name of Yahweh, let me attune to the vibrations of Orthoclase."* Slowly repeat these words to yourself three times. Soon you will begin to sense a state of calm, and sensations of serene security will begin to fill your consciousness. Allow yourself to merge with the vibrations amplified through Orthoclase, and feel yourself tapping into the beauty and tranquil understanding of your own intuitive wisdom. Allow yourself to experience the warm, comforting sensations and the visual representations of Divine Light Energy Transmission afforded by your Orthoclase Crystal. Allow yourself to know the unrivaled, unquestioned sanctity of evolved heart chakra energy states. Allow yourself to experience the wonder and the benevolence of Peace within The Wisdom of One.

4.

When you are ready to return from your Orthoclase Meditation, count backwards from ten to one. At the count of one, open your eyes and breathe deeply several times. *(It is most important that you give yourself adequate time to reintegrate after this Meditation. Breathe deeply for one to three minutes.) REMAIN SEATED.* Continue deep breathing until you begin to feel grounded within the reality of your Meditation room. *REMAIN SEATED.* Do not be in a hurry to move from your seated position. Reflect upon your Meditation experience and savor the sense of Tranquility and gentleness that fills you with a sense of assurance and understanding. Be at Peace within The Wisdom of One.

PERIDOT MEDITATION

Peridot amplifies a pure, radiant green ray that transmits dynamic, facilitating Earth energy to all systems of the human body. Directed toward affecting the dynamics and function of the heart chakra, but being influenced by the yellow ray within its green vibration, Peridot also acts to facilitate optimum function of organ systems associated with the solar plexus and the navel chakras. Further, Peridot lends significant assistance to the efficient operation and regeneration of the immune system.

Many will find that wearing Peridot or Clear Quartz Crystal pendants with Peridot cabochons will initiate a general sense of well-being, while simultaneously generating a higher level of resistance to both infection and bodily dysfunction. Quite inexpensive in the natural or tumbled state, Peridot is readily available from Rock Shops and Jewelers who offer a wide selection of rings, pendants, necklaces and earrings of Peridot.

1.

To prepare for your Peridot Meditation, select three tumbled or natural Peridot specimens. Cleanse and bless your Peridot and situate yourself in an upright position in a quiet, softly illuminated room.

2.

Begin your Meditation by initiating a rhythmic breathing sequence. Inhale deeply through your nose, hold the breath for three seconds and exhale from your mouth. As you inhale, visualize cleansing Golden/White Light Vibrations entering your nose, traveling down your trachea, filling your lungs, chest cavity and heart center with glowing LoveLight Vibrations. As you exhale, visualize tension, frustration and anger leaving your body in dark, cloudy swirls of energy. Bless yourself and your discordant vibrations in The Name of Yahweh, by The Spirit of Christ Jesus, as you cast this dissonant energy unto the ether to find Peaceful resolution. Continue the rhythmic breathing until you feel that your body has become totally relaxed (*usually, relaxation is accomplished within three to five minutes*).

3.

Now, pick up your Peridot Crystals in your left hand and begin to gaze upon them. As you gaze upon your Crystals, gently stroke the Crystals with the index finger of your right hand and silently repeat these words, *"Attune to the green ray of Peridot. Attune. Attune. Attune to the green ray of Peridot."* Repeat these words several times. Soon you may begin to feel tingling or sensations of warmth in your hands, fingers and arms. This is the signal that your energy matrix is aligning with the energy being amplified through the Peridot Crystals.

4.

Visually fix the color of Peridot in your mind. Close your eyes and repeat to yourself, *"Attune, Balance, Integrate, Ground."*

Repeat these words several times, as you watch the green ray of Peridot growing stronger in your mind. Now, visualize the energy of Peridot as a glowing, green sphere residing at your heart chakra. See the green ray of Peridot as it fills your heart chakra with transformational energy born of Mother Earth. Feel the radiant, green sphere of Peridot as it warms your heart center, filling you with a sense of vitality and rejuvenation.

From the center of the green sphere residing at your heart chakra, visualize a green arrow that emerges and follows your chakra cord down to your solar plexus. When the arrow reaches your solar plexus, visualize the tip of the green arrow as it grows and transforms into a green sphere that fills your solar plexus area with the green ray of Peridot. Now you have glowing, green spheres of Peridot at both your heart and solar plexus chakras. Hold this visualization and feel the warm, pulsating vibrations that fill you. Allow yourself to be bathed by the transforming Divine Light Vibration amplified through your Peridot Crystals.

Now, from the center of the green sphere that fills your solar plexus, visualize a green arrow that comes forth to travel down your chakra cord to your navel center. When the arrow reaches your navel chakra, watch the tip of the green arrow as it transforms into a radiant, green sphere that fills your navel center with the green ray of Peridot. And now you have the benevolent ray of Peridot alive within you, glowing in green spheres residing at your heart, solar plexus and navel chakras. Hold this visualization and feel the vibrant energy of Peridot's green ray as it sends waves of LoveLight Vibrations along your chakra cord.

5.

When you are ready to return to the reality of your Meditation room, simply count backwards from ten to one. At the count of one, open your eyes and breathe deeply several times. Remain seated and feel the freshness, the deep sense of invigoration that fills you. Reflect upon your Peridot Meditation and know that you have connected with the very heart of Mother Earth's nurturing vibration. Allow yourself to remain in Peaceful communion with the vibrations of Mother Earth, as you now channel your Love to Her in appreciation for Her Loving Kindness.

(Note: This Meditation can be performed in a reclined position with equal efficiency. Using natural or tumbled Peridot specimens, simply place one Crystal upon each chakra prior to visualizing the green ray of Peridot as a green sphere residing at the heart, then the solar plexus and finally the navel chakras.)

PHANTOM QUARTZ MEDITATION

Phantom Quartz Crystals are Clear or Smoky Quartz Crystals with Chlorite or Magnesite veils that form characteristic triangular or pyramidal structures within the shaft of the Crystal. Other Crystals can be found with Chlorite and/or Magnesite inclusions forming what may appear to be landscapes within the Crystal. These Crystals are also classed with Phantom Crystals, but are further classified as Chlorite or Magnesite included Crystals. Quite spectacular in appearance, Phantom Quartz Crystals most often display veils in white, green, blue and red.

Phantom Quartz Crystals offer mankind the opportunity of viewing human evolution in terms of stages or layers of consciousness that produce patterns of behavior. Once behavioral foundations or "karmic memories" are established and identified, fairly accurate predictions can be made regarding behavior tendencies. By investigating the underlying factors or layers of consciousness, one can identify areas of dysfunction that adversely impact upon one's entire perception of mortal existence and subsequent behavior patterns. With the aid of Phantom Quartz Crystals, the soul incarnate can learn to penetrate the layers of consciousness that hold the keys to problematic attitudes and behaviors, and transmute the areas of discordance that impede the evolutionary journey of the soul.

Phantom Quartz Crystals are readily available from New Age and Rock Shops in a wide range of sizes and prices. Be prepared though, because the base price for Phantom Quartz Crystals is significantly higher than either Clear or Smoky Quartz Crystals. Nevertheless, from both the standpoints of sheer beauty as well as being a most dynamic tool for mankind's evolving consciousness, a well-formed Phantom Crystal is certainly worth the additional expense.

1.

To prepare for your Phantom Quartz Crystal Meditation, select a Phantom Crystal that literally "calls out to you". This will be a specimen whose Phantom appearance will totally captivate you, compelling you to look deeper and deeper inside the shaft of the Crystal. After selecting your Crystal, cleanse and bless the Crystal in the prescribed manner before proceeding.

2.

To begin your Meditation, select a softly illuminated, quiet room and seat yourself in an upright manner. Begin your rhythmic breathing sequence by inhaling through the nose and slowly exhaling from the mouth. As you inhale, visualize cleansing Golden/White Light Energy entering your nose, traveling down your trachea, filling your lungs and heart center with glowing LoveLight Sensations. As you exhale, visualize tension and stress, frustration and hostility leaving your body in dark, cloudy swirls of dissonant energy. Now, bless yourself and your discordant vibrations in The Name of Yahweh, by The Spirit of Christ Jesus, as you cast these disruptive vibrations unto the ether to find Peace. Continue your rhythmic breathing until you feel completely relaxed.

3.

Now, pick up your Phantom Quartz Crystal in your left hand and begin to gaze upon it. With the index finger of your right hand, gently stroke the side of your Crystal and silently repeat the words, *"Attune, Balance, Integrate, Ground."* Repeat these words several times and allow yourself to merge with the dynamics of the Phantom appearance. At this time you may begin to experience warm, tingling sensations in your hands, fingers, arms and third eye, which will signal that the attunement process is well under way.

4.

Now, say to yourself, *"In The Name of Yahweh, by The Spirit of Christ Jesus, let the layers of my consciousness be revealed to me. Let me merge with the layers of the Phantom Crystal and let my truth unfold."* Place the Phantom Crystal against your third eye center and visualize the triangular pattern entering your third eye perception. See the triangular pattern fill your third eye center and expand in size as the triangular pattern moves throughout your cranium. Feel the waves of energy pass through your third eye to clear away confusion and counterproductive thought patterns. Allow yourself to experience the quiet and calm of inner knowing. Allow yourself to see the reality of the layers of consciousness that make you think, feel and act as you do.

At this time, many experience visual representations of behaviors that illustrate the kinds of patterns that have formed the layers of one's unconsciousness. Relax and allow the visions to unfold, as you will be shown the areas of your consciousness

193

that require transmutation, forgiveness of self or blessing. Allow yourself to see the truth of your reality and know that by accepting truth you have taken the first step toward resolving karmic debts that lay buried within the layers of your consciousness.

5.

When you are ready to return from your Phantom Quartz Meditation, simply count backwards from ten to one. At the count of one, *REMAIN SEATED AND DO NOT OPEN YOUR EYES*. Breathe deeply several times, inhaling through your nose and slowly exhaling from your mouth. Again, count backwards from ten to one. At the count of one, open your eyes and remain seated. Do not be in a hurry to move about. Rather, remain seated as you reflect upon your Meditation, making note of those areas of your consciousness that require attention.

RHODOCROSITE MEDITATION

Rhodocrosite is a most important stone for this time in mortal evolution, for Rhodocrosite amplifies a rich salmon pink Divine Light Vibration that aids in integrating the energies of the upper and lower chakra triads by assisting in the assimilation of spiritual and emotional energies into the dynamics of physical reality. Rhodocrosite impacts upon the heart chakra and solar plexus center in an attempt to bridge the energies of these two strategic centers, thereby initiating balance between the higher and practical aspects of mortal existence.

Rhodocrosite is available in Crystal shops is many forms. From exquisite cut and polished cabochons, rings, pendants, necklaces and geometric shapes to tumbled, semi-tumbled and rough slabs, Rhodocrosite specimens can be found that will aesthetically appeal to and suit the budget of everyone.

1.

To begin your Rhodocrosite Meditation, situate yourself in a quiet, softly illuminated room in an upright position. Begin your rhythmic breathing sequence by inhaling through the nose and exhaling from the mouth. As you inhale, visualize cleansing Golden/White Light Vibrations entering your nose, filling your lungs and heart center, sending warm, glowing sensations throughout your body. As you slowly exhale, visualize tensions, anxieties, frustrations, angers and stress leaving your body in dark, cloudy swirls of discordant energy. Bless your discordant vibrations in The Name of Yahweh and cast them unto the ether to find Peace.

2.

Now, pick up your Rhodocrosite Crystal that you have cleansed and blessed *(cabochons, tumbled and semi-tumbled specimens are best for this Meditation)* with your left hand and begin to gaze upon it. Silently, repeat these words to yourself several times, *"Attune, Balance, Integrate, Ground."* Now, begin to stroke your Rhodocrosite Crystal with the index finger of your right hand and say to yourself, *"Attune to the vibrations of Rhodocrosite. Attune. Attune. Attune to the vibrations of Rhodocrosite."* Repeat these statements three times. After a time you may start to experience a warming or tingling sensation in your hands, fingers and arms. You may also experience energy surges within your chakra centers, especially your heart and solar plexus or navel centers. Continue your rhythmic breathing.

3.

Now, close your eyes and visualize the color of Rhodocrosite filling your heart center. See the radiant salmon pink ray of Rhodocrosite grow brighter, more vibrant as it pulsates stronger and stronger at your heart center.

Next, visualize a salmon pink beam leaving from the center of your Rhodocrosite-colored heart chakra and traveling down to your solar plexus chakra. When the beam reaches your solar plexus, visualize your solar plexus center as it begins to fill up with the salmon pink ray of Rhodocrosite. See your solar plexus chakra begin to glow with the same salmon pink intensity as your heart chakra.

Visualize a second salmon pink beam that leaves from the center of the solar plexus and travels upward to the heart chakra. Watch as your heart and solar plexus centers find balance in their rate of vibration, as the salmon pink beam from the heart center feeds the solar plexus while simultaneously the salmon pink beam of the solar plexus center feeds the heart chakra.

Now, say to yourself, *"Let there be integration and balance of all things that live within me."* Savor the vibrations that fill you. Feel yourself moving toward a more harmonious inner being. Know that the Blessings of Serenity and Peace are indeed the birthright of all Creation. Know that by The Grace of The God, all things are as One.

4.

When you are ready to terminate your Rhodocrosite Meditation, slowly count backwards from ten to one. At the count of one, open your eyes and breathe deeply several times. Do not be in a hurry to move about; rather, savor the LoveLight Vibrations that fill you with Peace and contentment, and reflect upon your Meditation.

ROSE QUARTZ MEDITATION

Rose Quartz Crystals reflect the warm, facilitating pink ray of The Divine Light Spectrum, and the gift that Rose Quartz bestows is particularly directed for use at the heart center *(4th chakra)*, where traumatic memories and emotional wounds may lie festering for many lifetimes. By infusing The Divine Light Vibrations of Rose Quartz Crystals into the heart center, emotional wounds and memories can be resolved and transmuted, thereby allowing the opening of the heart center for the true, altruistic, benevolent expression of Love.

Many times, the emotional traumas sustained in life severely impact upon the mind and body, causing one's self-esteem to dwindle or in some cases, self-esteem is never given an opportunity to develop at all. Abusive relationships, failures to excel academically, peer pressures, inability to land a satisfying job or inability to advance one's job status and many other factors and/or conditions influence one's perceptions and sense of self-worth.

Frequently, these emotional conditions and factors damage and become attached to the heart center in such a way as to cause the heart center to require shielding or protection. Subsequently, the heart center closes, making the individual less cognizant of external factors that might cause further wounding, as well as blinding the individual to the reasons that trigger intense reactionary behavior when confronted by situations that are perceived to be threatening. This closing of the heart center makes it difficult, if not impossible, for the individual to feel good about him/herself as being a valuable, productive person who is worthy of Love and consideration, and further lessens the possibility of the individual being able to give Love, in the purest state of Divine Light Vibration, to another person.

Rose Quartz Crystal Meditation can repair the damaged, closed heart center, and allow the individual to grow emotionally. This Meditation can also aid in the repair and recovery process of stress-related dysfunctions that impact directly upon the heart muscle as well. *(In cases of hypertension, heart disease, heart attack, stroke, heart palpitations and other coronary/heart conditions, dietary, hereditary and environmental factors must also be addressed to effect systemic transformation.)*

Select a Rose Quartz Crystal, a natural specimen, a tumbled Crystal or a cut, polished shape that appeals to you. Exquisite terminated Rose Quartz Crystals are available, but are quite expensive. These terminated specimens are primarily mined from one South American location, but soon these Crystals will be discovered in other regions, making them readily available to the public and more affordable.

1.

After cleansing and blessing your Crystal, seat yourself in a quiet, softly illuminated room and center yourself. Hold the Crystal in your left hand, cradling your left hand with your right hand. Gaze upon your Crystal, focusing upon the warm, gentle ray of Rose Quartz. Then consciously say to yourself, *"Attune to the pink ray of Rose Quartz. Attune. Attune. Attune to the pink ray of Rose Quartz."* Repeat these statements several times and relax, as the attunement process has begun.

2.

Now, begin your rhythmic breathing, inhaling through your nose and exhaling from your mouth. As you inhale, visualize the pink ray of your Rose Quartz Crystal traveling in through your nose with each breath, filling your chest and lungs and then moving directly into your heart center. Breathe deeply and watch as the benevolent pink ray fills your chest cavity with the warming, comforting sensations of Love. Breathe deeply and savor the soft, consoling pink vibrations. As you exhale, visualize all tension, stress and emotional discordance leaving your body in dark, cloudy swirls of energy that you expel from your mouth. Bless your discordant energies in The Name of Yahweh, by The Spirit of The Christ, as you cast these energies unto the ether to find Peace.

3.

As you move deeper into your Meditation, your breathing will become progressively more shallow. You will experience tingling, warming, invigorating sensations that fill you with a new appreciation for life. You will feel the radiance of the pink ray gently pulsing within your heart center, purposeful in its intent to transform and transmute emotional traumas into glowing sensations of LoveLight Energy. See the shimmering pink ray of Rose Quartz as it becomes more and more centered, vibrating at your heart chakra. Now, visualize the pink ray of Rose Quartz spreading from your heart chakra to fill your entire body with glowing sensations. Visualize yourself radiating with the pink ray from head to toe. Feel your body in attunement with your Rose Quartz Crystal, vibrating with the benevolent pink ray, as you choose to develop positive feelings, generating self-Love, self-worth and Love for all mankind, and see that there is indeed hope for a better life-condition. Feel your body radiating with the gentle glow of Rose Quartz, and know that now you are being embraced in The Loving Arms of God.

4.

When you are ready to end your Rose Quartz Meditation, simply count backwards from ten to one. At the count of one, open your eyes and breathe deeply several times. Remain seated and savor the warm, glowing sensations that fill you.

SELENITE MEDITATION

Clear Selenite Crystals stimulate the crown *(7th)* chakra energy center, allowing the precepts of Higher Consciousness to develop in the conscious mind. Selenite opens the passageway between Spiritual Wisdom and the Earthly comprehension and application of Universal Law by infusing the conscious mind with the dynamics and motivations *(the Golden/White Light Vibration)* of the etheric self. The pure Golden/White Light Vibration amplified through Clear Selenite Crystals elevates the conscious mind to realms beyond third dimension form and thought processes and aids the dedicated practitioner in gathering Universal Knowledge that greatly impacts upon improving third dimension reality.

Selenite Crystals appear in many different shapes and color varieties, which determine the most appropriate use and illustrate the versatility of Selenite. Clear and frosty Selenite clusters, arrowhead and fishtail forms are best used as Meditation Partners, and many specimens are known to have been encoded with alchemal information, as well as information relating to the developmental changes of Mother Earth. Many who diligently attempt to attune to the vibrations of Selenite are able to access the information stored in these Crystals. Water-included Selenite Crystals *(these are Crystals that have small pockets of water with air-bubbles floating within them formed within the crystalline matrix)* also make excellent Meditation Partners, but are rarely encountered and quite expensive. Clear Selenite Wands and Spears are used by Light-workers to channel Golden/White Light Vibrations into the crown chakra, thereby aiding in the comprehension and assimilation of Spiritual Truth.

Selenite Rosettes appear in shades of light brown and can be used as aids in past life regression. Selenite Rosettes resemble the human brain and by focusing and attuning to these Crystals *(which may measure one to twelve inches in diameter)* one is able to access ancient memories and problematic behavior patterns that subconsciously impact upon present thoughts and behaviors. By addressing and understanding the underlying motivations for our thoughts and behaviors, we are able to break karmic patterns that result in dysfunctional and/or counterproductive behaviors.

1.

To prepare for your Selenite Meditation, select a Clear Selenite Crystal that both intuitively and intrinsically appeals to you. After cleansing and blessing your Crystal, study the shape and the layered formation of your Crystal. Observe any inclusions that may be present within your Crystal *(white lines and/or triangular patterns that are set at an angle to the linear growth of the Crystal).*

(NOTE: *As with all Crystal Meditations and especially so with Selenite Meditation, it is strongly advised that The LoveLight Prayer/Invocation, The 23rd Psalm and Affirmations are performed prior to engaging in the Selenite Meditation.)*

2.

To begin your Meditation, situate yourself in an upright position in a quiet, dimly lit room. Inhale deeply through your nose and slowly exhale from your mouth. As you inhale, visualize cleansing Golden/White Light Energy entering your nose, filling your lungs, chest cavity and heart center. As you exhale, visualize tension, anxiety, frustration, anger and stress leaving your body through your mouth in dark, cloudy swirls of energy. Bless your discordant vibrations in The Name of Yahweh and send these vibrations unto the ether to find Peaceful resolution. Continue your deep breathing until you feel relaxed.

3.

Now, pick up your Selenite Crystal in your left hand. Place your right beneath your left hand and cradle your Crystal in your lap. Begin to gaze deeply into your Selenite Crystal. Now, silently say to yourself, *"Attune to the vibrations of Selenite. Attune. Attune. Attune to the Golden/White Light Vibration of Selenite."* Repeat these words several times. After a time, you may begin to feel your Selenite Crystal becoming warm and throbbing in your hands. Shortly thereafter, you may experience tingling sensations in your fingers, hands and arms.

When the physical sensations begin (or after holding and gazing upon your Crystal for ten minutes, whichever comes first), slowly raise your Selenite Crystal with your left hand and place it against your crown chakra for sixty seconds. As the Selenite touches your crown chakra, you will experience an energy influx that expands and clears your crown chakra. This tingling sensation is the transmission of Golden/White Light Energy through your Selenite into your crown chakra.

4.

Remove the Selenite Crystal from your crown chakra and place it against your third eye center for up to five minutes. While holding the Selenite against your third eye center, silently repeat to yourself, *"Attune, Balance, Integrate, Ground."* As you repeat these words, you will experience energy movements from your crown chakra to your base chakra. Relax and allow your journey into Light-mindedness to unfold. You may experience visual references to ancient civilizations and distant lands, references designed to unlock the Knowledge and Wisdom of your intuitive self. You may also experience episodes of conscious channeling or find yourself in an altered state, traveling through the cosmos, conversing with Light-beings. Individual results and experiences vary, but for those who are diligent and patient, Selenite can open the door to enlightenment beyond measure.

5.

When you are ready to return to the reality of your Meditation room, slowly count backwards from ten to one. When you reach one, *REMAIN SEATED AND DO NOT OPEN YOUR EYES.* Now, visualize your feet as being the roots of a towering oak tree, reaching through the floor and sinking deep into Mother Earth. Now, silently say to yourself, *"Attune, Balance, Integrate, Ground."* Repeat these words several times and hold the visualization of yourself firmly rooted into Mother Earth for three to five minutes. Once again, slowly count backwards from ten to one. When you reach one, open your eyes and remain seated. Breathe deeply several times, inhaling through your nose and exhaling from your mouth. You will feel very relaxed yet invigorated and you will be fully grounded in third dimension reality.

SMITHSONITE MEDITATION

Smithsonite is a Crystalline Zinc Carbonate form found in several parts of the world, including The United States. Amplifying Divine Light Vibrations in shades of yellow, lavender, purple, turquoise, pale blue or green and silvery gray, Smithsonite's appearance upon the Earth Plane is designed to assist mankind in the integration of the etheric, mental and emotional bodies. The result of Smithsonite's integration function facilitates mankind's conscious understanding of the elements of human emotions, thereby enabling mankind to identify and transmute problematic, counterproductive and/or discordant emotional patterns.

The different color varieties of Smithsonite impact upon the solar plexus, heart, throat, third eye and crown chakras in affecting integration and alignment of creative, emotional, intellectual and etheric energies: silvery gray - crown chakra; lavender/purple - third eye chakra; turquoise/pale blue - throat chakra; pale green - heart chakra; yellow - solar plexus chakra. Smithsonite has appeared at this stage of mortal evolution to assist in the final stages of emotional/etheric/mental resolution, which will allow mortal man to finally comprehend the core motivations that have compelled and incited discordant behavior patterns throughout karmic history.

Readily available from most Crystal dealers and Rock Shops, Smithsonite can be found in natural slabs and clusters that range in size from a few ounces to several pounds. Allow your intuition to guide you in choosing the color and type of Crystal formation suitable for your needs.

1.

To prepare for your Smithsonite Meditation, select a Crystal that you can easily hold in the palm of your hand, one that is a color variety that literally calls out to you. Cleanse and bless your Smithsonite in advance, so that you can quickly settle into your Meditation.

2.

To begin your Smithsonite Meditation, situate yourself in a quiet, softly illuminated room in an upright position, then initiate a rhythmic breathing sequence by inhaling deeply through the nose and slowly exhaling from the mouth. As you inhale, visualize cleansing Golden/White Light Vibrations entering your nose, traveling down your trachea, filling your lungs, chest cavity and heart center with glowing LoveLight Sensations. As you exhale, visualize tension, stress, frustration and angers leaving your body as you expel dark, cloudy swirls of energy from your mouth. Now, bless yourself and your discordant energy in The Name of Yahweh, by The Spirit of Christ Jesus, as you cast this dissonant energy unto the ether to find Peaceful resolution.

3.

Now, pick up your Smithsonite Crystal in your left hand and begin to gaze upon it. Notice the interesting Crystalline formation and the gentle yet captivating color displayed by your Smithsonite. Stroke your Smithsonite with the index finger of your right hand and repeat to yourself, *"Attune to the vibrations of Smithsonite. Attune. Attune. Attune to the vibrations of Smithsonite."* Repeat these words several times. Soon you may begin to experience warm, tingling sensations in your hands and fingers, and surges of energy along your chakra cord as well.

4.

Visually fix the color of your Smithsonite Crystal in your mind. Close your eyes and repeat the words, *"Attune, Balance, Integrate, Ground."* Say these words several times to usher in the integration mode of etheric, mental and emotional energies. Now, visualize the color of your Smithsonite as a swirling energy mass three feet above your head. See the pastel color of Smithsonite swirling above your head, then watch as the irregularly shaped mass of color slowly transforms and becomes a radiant sphere of Smithsonite. From the center of the Smithsonite sphere, watch as a beam of pastel color emerges and travels downward to penetrate your crown chakra. Feel the energy surge as your crown chakra is opened and invigorated by the Smithsonite beam. Watch as the Smithsonite beam slowly travels the length of your chakra cord, from crown to base, energizing and opening each chakra along the way. Feel the glowing sensations that fill your chakra cord and chakra centers. Now, allow the vibrations and color of Smithsonite to expand from your chakra centers and cord to fill your entire body. Savor the sense of Harmony and Peace that you have achieved. Feel the communion and sense the cooperative balance between etheric, mental and emotional energies that has taken place. Allow yourself to sense and appreciate the resolution of emotional conflicts that is under way. Release yourself from guilt and self-abasement. Feel your personal connection to The

Infinite Body of God. Allow self this moment to free yourself from debilitating emotional and reactionary behaviors, and understand that everything is good in The Light of One.

5.

When you are ready to end your Smithsonite Meditation, slowly count backwards from ten to one. At the count of one, open your eyes and breathe deeply several times. *REMAIN SEATED.* Do not be in a hurry to move about. Give yourself ample time to reintegrate into third dimension reality. Remain seated and reflect upon your Meditation experience.

SMOKY QUARTZ MEDITATION

Smoky Quartz Crystals range in color intensity from the palest, transparent hues of brown to some of the richest, earthiest shades of brown encountered in the Quartz/Mineral Kingdom. These Crystals are endowed with the ability to amplify and channel the purest of the brown color spectrum into the base *(1st)* chakra to assist the individual in establishing and maintaining a "grounded state" in the physical plane. What this means is that Smoky Quartz Crystals reflect a color of The Divine Light Vibration that when attuned to and infused into the base chakra enables the individual to connect with, comprehend and focus upon the dynamics of Earthly life. The brown ray of Smoky Quartz Crystals aids the individual in attaining a centered state of being that nurtures one's ability to see, appreciate and make contributions to the realities of Earthly existence. By attuning to the vibrations inherent to Smoky Quartz, mankind is given a greater opportunity to render unto our brethren and Mother Earth the practical understanding of Universal Law by which all things derive Love and Peace.

The choices of Smoky Quartz Crystals suitable for use in Meditation are many. Not only is there a wide range of color intensities to choose from, but there are many spectacular inclusions that can be found in Smoky Quartz. Many Smoky Quartz specimens are found with golden needles, or rutiles, crisscrossing within the shaft of the Crystal. Rutilated Smoky Quartz, as these Crystals are called, possess, in addition to the brown ray, the intensity of the gold ray that contributes to establishing the Higher Consciousness Vibration of the crown chakra *(7th chakra)*. In essence, Rutilated Smoky Quartz Crystals act to channel Spiritual Conscience and Earthly reality simultaneously, thereby aiding in producing a state of mind essential to the execution of Universal Law.

Smoky Quartz Crystals can also display brilliant rainbows that reflect many different color combinations that enhance the vibration of the brown ray, and frequently, Smoky Quartz Crystals are found with unique Chlorite inclusions that resemble landscapes, mountains and glacial formations. Chlorite inclusions that form triangular or pyramidal shapes within some of these Crystals, know as "phantoms", will be discussed in the section entitled "Phantom Quartz Meditations". Smoky Quartz Crystals from the Himalayas have a characteristic icy appearance, as if these Crystals had been formed to resemble the ice-capped mountains from which they come.

1.

Select either a natural Smoky Quartz Generator, a tumbled Crystal or a cut, faceted, polished shape that appeals to you. After cleansing and blessing your Crystal, situate yourself in an upright position in a quiet, dimly lit room. Relax yourself by beginning your rhythmic sequence, inhaling through your nose and exhaling from your mouth.

Hold your Crystal and begin gazing upon it. Notice the unique characteristics of your Crystal, its color intensity, its internal formations, the shape and size of its faceting. Continue your rhythmic breathing. Close your eyes and say to yourself,

"Attune to the vibrations of Smoky Quartz. Attune. Attune. Attune to the grounding brown ray of Smoky Quartz." Slowly repeat these statements several times, until a tingling, warming vibration begins to rise in your body.

2.

After a time, you will feel the vibrations of your Smoky Quartz Crystal entering you, settling into your base chakra. Feel the vibrations growing stronger, moving from your base chakra down your legs into your feet, as if your body were the trunk of a tree and the vibrations were roots being sunk deeply into Mother Earth. *(Your breathing will have become shallow by this time.)* See yourself with the brown ray of Smoky Quartz filling your pelvic region, then your legs and feet, connecting you with vital Earth energy, supporting you to withstand the rigors of daily life, much the same as Mother Earth strengthens and supports the towering oak to withstand the siege of storms and turmoil. Feel yourself charged by the brown ray of Smoky Quartz, filled with the conviction to weather any storm and to see the true reality of your Earthly condition. Know that the strength of conviction of Divine Truth is yours to utilize in the cognition and execution of your mortal responsibilities. And know too that your blessed connection to Mother Earth is being nurtured with and grounded in Love, Peace and Prosperity.

3.

When you are ready to return to the reality of your Meditation room, slowly count backwards from ten to one. At the count of one, open your eyes and breathe deeply several times. Remain seated until you feel fully integrated in third dimension.

SUGILITE MEDITATION

Sugilite, also known as Luvulite, amplifies a deeply soothing purple ray of The Divine Light Spectrum. Going beyond the calming sensations amplified by the purple ray of Amethyst, Sugilite impacts upon the crown and third eye chakras with the intent of balancing the activities of the pineal and pituitary glands, thereby providing an integral state of balance between the spiritual and emotional bodies. Sugilite in effect is capable of softening man's perceptions of the often harsh realities of third dimension existence that mankind experiences and allows to adversely affect the quality of daily life. With its ability to restore conscious understanding of third dimension realities, Sugilite offers itself as an aid in establishing and maintaining a functional perspective regarding the pitfalls encountered along the journey of life.

Sugilite commands a rather high price in the marketplace, but is available in a variety of forms. From natural and semi-tumbled specimens to pendants, necklaces and earrings, Sugilite can be found in most New Age or Rock & Mineral Shops. *(For the purpose of your Sugilite Meditation, a natural or semi-tumbled specimen that will comfortably rest in the palm of your hand is recommended.)*

1.

To prepare for your Sugilite Meditation, cleanse and bless your Sugilite specimen using the water/sunlight technique or by smudging or with prayer. *(To heighten your ability to merge with your Sugilite, after cleansing and blessing, rub a small amount of Essential Oil into the stone. As you rub and handle your Sugilite, you will feel the attunement process taking place.)*

2.

Begin your Meditation by situating yourself in an upright position in a quiet, softly illuminated room. Begin your rhythmic breathing sequence by inhaling through the nose and exhaling from the mouth. As you inhale, visualize cleansing Golden/White Light Vibrations entering your lungs, passing down your trachea, filling your lungs, chest cavity and heart center with warm, glowing LoveLight Sensations. As you exhale, visualize discordant energy, stress, tension, frustration and anger, leaving your body in dark, cloudy, swirling vibrations. Bless yourself and your discordant vibrations in The Name of Yahweh, by The Spirit of Christ Jesus, as you cast these disruptive, hostile energies unto the ether to find Peaceful resolution.

3.

Now, pick up your Sugilite specimen in your left hand and begin to gaze upon it, stroking the stone with the index finger of your right hand. Say to yourself, *"Attune to the purple ray of Sugilite. Attune. Attune. Attune to the purple ray of Sugilite."* Repeat these words several times. Visually fix the color of your Sugilite in your mind. Close your eyes and repeat to yourself,

"Attune, Balance, Integrate, Ground." By this time, you may have begun to experience tingling and sensations of warmth in your hands and fingers. Allow yourself to fully merge with your Sugilite specimen by again repeating the words, *"Attune, Balance, Integrate, Ground."*

4.

Now, visualize a large sphere that is the color of Sugilite hovering twelve inches above your head. See the Sugilite colored sphere above your head as it begins to slowly rotate in a clockwise manner. Now, watch as the Sugilite sphere slowly begins to descend and gently penetrates your crown chakra. Feel the soothing yet uplifting sensations that now are filling your crown chakra and moving toward your third eye center. See the rotating sphere of Sugilite as it now moves to fill your third eye with the resolution for achieving balanced states of perception. Feel the soothing, beneficent purple ray of Sugilite as it fills your entire cranium with a sense of order, Peace and gentle conviction. Feel the purple ray of Sugilite as it works to facilitate the integration of Spiritual Conscience with the reality of emotion. Allow yourself to float within the purple ray of Sugilite and find the contentment awaiting you that is the resolution of The Wisdom of One.

5.

When you are ready to disengage from your Sugilite Meditation, simply count backwards from ten to one. At the count of one, open your eyes and remain seated. Allow yourself the time to reflect upon and savor the sense of fulfillment and Peace that fills you. Be at Peace and know that within you is an abiding sense of Harmony that will work to balance and/or

217

counterbalance inclinations toward reactionary emotional episodes. Be at Peace within The Conscience of One.

TIGER EYE MEDITATION

Tiger Eye is a Quartz Silicate Mineral that amplifies colors of gold, green, blue, brown and black that impact upon the navel and upper base chakra areas by channeling crown chakra energies *(golden ray)* into the navel and upper base chakras for the purpose of facilitating the development and expression of Divine Will upon the Earth Plane. Tiger Eye's shimmering iridescence shows mankind that the golden ray of Divine Truth can comfortably coexist and naturally finds Harmony with grounding vibrations associated with the darker colors. This blending of crown chakra energies with vibrations designed to assist survival modes is what gives Tiger Eye its unique ability to guide mankind toward more balanced, conscionable behavior patterns in the treatment of all things born of Creation. Tiger Eye and especially Multi-Tiger Eye, which amplifies more blues and black vibrations along with the golden ray, channel crown chakra energies designed to acquaint mankind with the nature and purpose of the higher self and to assist man in identifying and activating the enduring constructs of Love, Serenity, Compassion, Mercy, Patience and Wisdom in every aspect of mortal existence.

Tiger Eye is mined in several locations around the world, and is readily available in a variety of forms at reasonable prices. For this Meditation, however, a tumbled, polished specimen or preferably a small sphere of Tiger Eye is recommended.

1.

To begin your Tiger Eye Meditation, situate yourself in an upright position in a quiet, softly illuminated room. Begin your rhythmic breathing sequence by inhaling deeply through the nose and slowly exhaling from the mouth. As you inhale, visualize radiant Golden/White Light Vibrations entering your nose, passing down your trachea, filling your lungs, chest cavity and heart center with warm, glowing LoveLight Sensations. As you exhale, visualize discordant vibrations leaving your body in dark, cloudy swirls of energy. Bless yourself and your discordant vibrations in The Name of Yahweh, by The Spirit of Christ Jesus, as you cast this dissonant energy unto the ether to find Peace.

2.

Now, pick up your Tiger Eye specimen *(that you have cleansed and blessed in advance)* with your left hand and begin to gaze upon it. Stroke your Tiger Eye with the index finger of your right hand as you repeat to yourself, *"Attune to the vibrations of Tiger Eye. Attune. Attune. Attune to the vibrations of Tiger Eye."* Slowly repeat these words to yourself several times. As you gaze upon your Tiger Eye, visually fix the colors and the interplay of the colors of your Tiger Eye in your mind. Now, close your eyes and silently repeat, *"Attune, Balance, Integrate, Ground."* Slowly repeat these words several times. Soon you may begin to experience warm, tingling sensations in your hands and fingers and movement along your chakra cord that will indicate that the attunement process has begun.

3.

Now, place your right hand upon your navel chakra *(about two inches below your navel)*. Hold your Tiger Eye in your left hand and slowly raise it to the level of the top of your head. Gently hold the Tiger Eye upon the top of your head at your crown chakra. Now, visualize the swirling, shimmering colors of your Tiger Eye above your head, moving to penetrate your crown chakra, traveling down your chakra cord and coming to rest and forming a shimmering sphere at your navel chakra. Watch the sphere of Tiger Eye at your navel chakra as it begins to slowly rotate in a clockwise manner. Feel the warm, glowing sensation that fills your navel chakra with an appreciation for and an understanding of "The Way" - Shambhala, the way of the Peaceful Warrior. Allow yourself to feel the contentment inherent to surrendering to the conscience of Divine Truth. Allow yourself to experience the integration of Divine Will with mortal existence. Allow yourself to be at Peace within The Oneness of Creation.

4.

When you are ready to return to the reality of your Meditation room, simply count backwards from ten to one. At the count of one, open your eyes, breathe deeply several times and remain seated. Reflect upon the sense of understanding that fills your consciousness. Feel the sense of wholeness that permeates you. Be at Peace and know that the conscience of all things great and small lives as One within you.

Plate 1. POLISHED FORMS: *(from left)* Smoky Quartz Point, Clear Quartz Point *(with rainbow)*, Rutilated Smoky Quartz Pyramid, Golden Citrine Point, Amethyst Point

Plate 2. (from top, clockwise) Smithsonite, Rhodocrosite in matrix, Wulfenite, Rhodocrosite, Kunzite, Sodalite, Amazonite

Plate 3. Adamite *(top)*, Ulexite *(bottom)*

223

Plate 4. CALCITES: *(Clockwise, from top):* Honey, Blue, Optical, Orange, Strawberry, Mango, Salmon, Green, White

Plate 5. *(Clockwise, from top)* Atacamite, Dolomite, Chalcopyrite, Kyanite Wing, Orthoclase

Plate 6. FLUORITES: *(Clockwise, from top)* Cluster, Octahedrons, Yittrium Fluorite

Plate 7. *(Clockwise, from top)* Emerald in matrix, Rhodonite, Barite, Amber, Rose Quartz

Plate 8. Apophyllite

Plate 9. Dioptase

Plate 10. Elestial Quartz Crystal

Plate 11. Celestite

225

Plate 12. (Clockwise, from top) Crystallized Petrified Wood, Petrified Wood *(Green Chromium inclusion)*, Petrified Figs, Petrified Wood

Plate 13. (Clockwise, from top) Lapis Lazuli Sphere, Crystallized Lapis in matrix, Pyrite Cubes, Pyrite, Natural Lapis, Pyrite

Plate 14. (Clockwise, from top) Marcasite/Sphalerite Slice, Chinese Fluorite with Pyrite, Goethite, Vanadanite, Ruby in matrix

Plate 15. (Clockwise, from top) Green Quartz, Herkimer Diamond, Double Terminated Red Quartz, Barite Crystal, Pink Halite

Plate 16. (from left) Brienzanite Sphere, Pampa Onyx Egg, Fossilized Marble Obelisk, Unakite Sphere, Rhyolite Sphere

Plate 17. (Clockwise, from top) Green Mica with Ruby, Pink Cobalt with Malachite, Azurite, Phenakite, Moss Malachite

Plate 18. (Clockwise, from top) Amethyst Cluster, Siberian Amethyst, Selenite Wand, Selenite Rosettes

227

Plate 19. *(Clockwise, from top)* Youngite, Azurite Nodule, Realgar, Danberite, Youngite

Plate 20. POLISHED MALACHITE FORMS: *(Clockwise, from top)* Pyramid, Obelisk, Massage Wands, Sphere

Plate 21. Shiva Lingams
(Tantric Meditation Stones)

Plate 22. *(Clockwise, from top)* Aquamarine, Lazulite, Kyanite Crystals, Imperial Topaz, Azulicite, Blue Apatite, Stibnite, Neptunite

228

Plate 23. (Clockwise, from top) Anhydrite, Garnet in matrix, Alunite, Lepidolite, Chrysocolla

Plate 24. OBSIDIAN: *(Clockwise, from top)* Rainbow, Snowflake, Mahogany, Apache Tears, Sheen Obsidian Sphere

Plate 25. METEORITES: *(Clockwise, from top)* Libya Glass, Tibetite, Tektite

Plate 26. (Clockwise, from top) Chrysocolla/Cuprite, Blue Kyanite, Aragonite, Peridot, Prehnite, Aragonite Cluster, Stilbite

Plate 27. *(Clockwise, from top)* Phantom Smoky Quartz, Aventurine, Citrine, Sunstones, Iolite, Paua Shell, Leopardskin Agate, Tourmalated Quartz, Bloodstone.

Plate 28. TOURMALINES: *(Clockwise, from top)* Watermelon in matrix, Tourmaline slice, Indicolite, Schorl, Elbaite, Rubellite

Plate 29. *(Clockwise, from top)* Epidote, Terminated Rose Quartz, Chrysoprase, Actinolite, Variscite, Onyx, Fire Agate.
(Center) Larimar

Plate 30. CABACHONS: *(Clockwise, from top)* Ammolite *(fossilized Mother of Pearl)*, Moonstones, Chrysocolla, Jade, Hematite, Sugilite, Tiger Eye, Malachite/Azurite, Covellite, Spectralite, Rutilated Quartz, Carnelian, Blue Lace Agate, Turquoise

TOURMALINE MEDITATION

Occurring in many different colors, Tourmaline Crystals are known to generate high electrical impulses and subsequently amplify some of the highest Divine Light Vibrations encountered in the Quartz/Mineral Kingdom. Exquisite Crystals mined in Brazil, Italy, Russia, Sri Lanka and The United States can be found in bi-color and tri-color formations, as well as in graduated shades of one color occurring throughout the length of the Crystal. Measuring only a few millimeters in length to specimens that measure several inches *(known as Tourmaline Wands)*, Tourmaline offers mankind a rainbow of Divine Light Vibration to assist in the journey of Soul Evolution. The following details the properties of the basic color formations most often encountered in Tourmaline Crystals.

DRAVITE (Brown Tourmaline): facilitates transmutation of discordant emotional energies from solar plexus and navel chakra; restores vital energy and grounding vibration to will power dynamics

ELBAITE (Green Tourmaline): transmits dynamic Earth energy that stimulates Healing Facilitation of both energy and organ systems of the body; distributed to entire body through the heart chakra, vibrations amplified through Elbaite serve to stimulate optimal functioning of the immune system

231

INDICOLITE (Blue Tourmaline): impacts upon third eye, throat and heart chakras in its various shades by removing blockages, opening chakras that have been closed due to emotional traumas, and infusing a pure, dynamic Divine Light Vibration into the energy system that soothes and facilitates well-being and promotes chakra balancing

RUBELLITE (Pink/Red Tourmaline): radiates vibrant Divine Light Energy directed toward the heart chakra, but brings Compassionate, nurturing vibration to any discordant system of the body; frequently found in combination with Green and/or Blue Tourmaline

SCHORL (Black Tourmaline): amplifies intense grounding vibration designed to repel and transmute dissonant energy systems from the base chakra; best applied with Clear and Smoky Quartz Crystals or utilized in Tourmalated Quartz

WATERMELON TOURMALINE (Green and Pink Tourmaline): stimulates dynamic systemic and emotionally facilitating vibrations for entire body; when sliced across the shaft of the Crystal, an outer layer colored green, then a clear white layer, then center pink/red colors are revealed

1.

For this Meditation, select a natural Tourmaline Crystal that appeals to your senses. The color of the Crystal you choose may well indicate that you are in need of facilitation/transmutation at the chakra that corresponds to the color of your Tourmaline Crystal. Allow your intuition to guide you in your selection.

After cleansing and blessing your Tourmaline Crystal, you are ready to begin your Tourmaline Meditation. Situate yourself in a seated position in a quiet, softly illuminated room. Begin your rhythmic breathing sequence by inhaling deeply through the nose, holding the breath for three seconds and slowly exhaling from the mouth. As you inhale, visualize cleansing Golden/White Light Vibrations entering your nose, traveling down your trachea, filling your chest cavity, lungs and heart center with glowing LoveLight Sensations. As you exhale, visualize tension, stress, frustration and anger leaving your body in dark, cloudy swirls of energy. Bless yourself and your discordant energy in The Name of Yahweh, by The Spirit of Christ Jesus, as you cast this dissonant energy unto the ether to find Peaceful resolution.

2.

Pick up your Tourmaline Crystal in your left hand and begin to gaze upon it. (If your Crystal is terminated, point the apex of the Crystal toward your body.) As you gaze upon the Crystal, silently repeat to yourself, *"Attune to the vibrations of Tourmaline. Attune. Attune. Attune to the_____ ray (fill in the blank with the appropriate color: pink, blue, etc.) of Tourmaline."* Now, close your eyes and gently stroke your Tourmaline Crystal with the index finger of your right hand and say to yourself, *"Attune, Balance, Integrate, Ground."* Repeat these words several times. After a short time, you will begin to experience sensations of warmth and tingling in your fingers, hands and arms.

3.

Now, with your left hand, place your Tourmaline Crystal directly upon the chakra that corresponds to its color vibration. Cradle your left hand with your right hand. Visualize the color of your Crystal entering your body and filling your chakra with the color of Tourmaline. See your chakra glowing with the color of your Tourmaline Crystal and feel the pulsing energy that fills your chakra. Hold this visualization for three to five minutes per Meditation.

4.

When you are ready to end your Tourmaline Meditation, simply count backwards from ten to one. At the count of one, open your eyes and breathe deeply several times. Remain seated. Reflect upon the dynamic energy that filled your body. Sense the deep nurturing, consoling vibrations that linger in your body as you reintegrate into third dimension reality. Allow yourself to gently float upon the energy systems of LoveLight Vibration. Allow yourself to reintegrate in conscious Harmony within yourself and with all things born of Creation. Allow yourself The Blessing of One.

TURQUOISE MEDITATION

Revered for its transformational qualities and as a complement to enlightened states of consciousness by Native American cultures, Turquoise amplifies light blue and light blue/green rays in The Divine Light Spectrum. It can be said that Turquoise facilitates the assimilation of Divine Truth and enables the expression of Etheric Wisdom in the spoken word. The gentle vibrations amplified through Turquoise can be felt warming the third eye, throat and/or heart chakras almost immediately upon handling the stone, providing a sense of confidence and conscious connection to life's dynamic truths. Further, the gift of Turquoise is said to be an act of Love and a wish for long life, health and prosperity.

Turquoise is available today in many forms of jewelry, but for this Meditation, natural Turquoise nuggets or slabs are recommended. Stabilized Turquoise that has been color-enhanced may appear more radiant, but natural specimens amplify purer energy transmissions.

1.

After cleansing and blessing your Turquoise *(the use of sea salts in the cleansing of Turquoise and other copper-related minerals will cause decomposition of the stone)* you are ready to begin your Turquoise Meditation.

2.

Situate yourself in an upright position in a quiet, softly illuminated room. Begin your rhythmic breathing sequence by inhaling through the nose and slowly exhaling from the mouth. As you inhale, visualize radiant Golden/White Light Vibrations entering your nose, traveling down your trachea, filling your lungs, chest cavity and heart center with warm, cleansing LoveLight Vibrations. As you exhale, visualize tension, frustration, stress and anger leaving your body in dark, cloudy swirls of energy. Bless yourself and your discordant vibrations in The Name of Yahweh, by The Spirit of Christ Jesus, as you cast these dissonant vibrations unto the ether to find Peaceful resolution.

3.

Now, pick up your Turquoise in your left hand and begin to gaze upon it. As you gaze upon the Turquoise, repeat these words to yourself, *"Attune to the vibrations of Turquoise. Attune. Attune. Attune to the blue ray of Turquoise."* With the index finger of your right hand, begin to stroke your Turquoise. Close your eyes and say to yourself, *"Attune, Balance, Integrate, Ground."* Repeat these words several times. Soon you may begin to experience tingling or warming sensations in your hands and fingers and within your chakra system as well.

4.

Allow yourself to merge deeper and deeper with the

vibrations amplified through your Turquoise. Now, visualize a sphere radiating with the blue ray of Turquoise that measures three feet in diameter hovering three feet above your head. Watch as the Turquoise sphere slowly begins to rotate and lower itself toward the top of your head. Watch as the Turquoise sphere gently penetrates your crown chakra and begins to color your cranium with the blue ray of Turquoise. See the sphere of Turquoise as it colors your third eye center with the blue ray and moves down your face filling your cheeks, nose and mouth areas with the blue ray of Turquoise. Watch as the Turquoise sphere colors your chin and moves to fill your throat chakra with the blue ray. Now, see your head and throat areas within the Turquoise sphere, as you watch the blue sphere move downward to fill your shoulders, upper chest and heart chakra with the blue ray of Turquoise.

Allow yourself to be caressed by the blue ray of Turquoise. Float within the tranquil sea of blue Turquoise that fills your upper torso. Hear, see, feel and be as One with The Divine Wisdom of Absolute Truth. Allow yourself to be at Peace.

5.

When you are ready to return from your Turquoise Meditation, simply count backwards from ten to one. At the count of one, open your eyes and breathe deeply several times. Remain seated. Reflect upon the deep sense of understanding that fills you. Relax and know that elements of Absolute Truth that once may have been beyond your ability to articulate are at the forefront of your consciousness now. Be at Peace and know that subsequent Turquoise Meditations will further heighten your understanding and ability to transmit The Wisdom of One. Be at Peace and know that all things are as One.

WULFENITE MEDITATION

Wulfenite occurs as a yellow or reddish-orange Crystalline Mineral, and is found in the oxidation zone of Lead deposits in numerous locations around the world. Wulfenite offers mankind amplified Divine Light Vibrations that impact upon the solar plexus and navel chakras, assisting in the purging of toxins from the spleen and digestive organs. Further, Wulfenite directs such vital Divine Light Vibrations into the human energy system that some bowel dysfunctions can be significantly improved with limited applications. And in its cleansing activity, Wulfenite serves to assist mankind in the release of discordant energy systems that adversely impact upon bodily functions on the cellular level *(that is, Wulfenite impacts upon metabolic functions: anabolism - the process by which food is changed into living tissue and catabolism - the process by which living tissue is changed into waste products of a simpler chemical composition)*. Wulfenite comes to mankind as a Crystalline brother eager to effect systemic changes that will enhance the process of Soul Evolution.

1.

To prepare for your Wulfenite Meditation, select a natural Wulfenite cluster that you can comfortably hold in the palm of your hand. Cleanse and bless your Wulfenite cluster in the prescribed manner in advance, so that you can settle into your Meditation quickly.

2.

To begin your Wulfenite Meditation, situate yourself in a quiet, softly illuminated room. Adopt either an upright, seated position or lie on the floor on your back. Begin your rhythmic breathing sequence by inhaling deeply through the nose, holding the breath for three seconds and slowly exhaling from the mouth. As you inhale, visualize cleansing Golden/White Light Vibrations entering your nose, traveling down your trachea, filling your lungs, chest cavity and heart center with glowing LoveLight Sensations. As you exhale, visualize tension, stress, frustration and hostility leaving your body in dark, cloudy swirls of energy. Now, bless yourself and your discordant energies in The Name of Yahweh, by The Spirit of Christ Jesus, as you cast your dissonant energies unto the ether to find Peaceful resolution.

3.

Now, pick up your Wulfenite cluster in your left hand and begin to gaze upon it. Say to yourself, *"Attune to the vibrations of Wulfenite. Attune. Attune. Attune to the vibrations of Wulfenite."* Gently stroke your Wulfenite cluster with the index finger of your right hand and silently repeat to yourself, *"Attune, Balance, Integrate, Ground."* Repeat these words several times. Soon you may begin to experience energy surges along your chakra cord.

4.

Now, place your Wulfenite cluster at your navel chakra *(about two inches below your navel)* with your left hand. Place your right hand over your left, so as to cradle your Wulfenite cluster at your navel chakra. Once again say to yourself, *"Attune, Balance, Integrate, Ground."* Repeat these words again and again. Soon you will begin to feel a warm, penetrating sensation at your navel chakra. This warm, glowing sensation will be that of the Wulfenite amplifying and transmitting Divine Light Vibrations into your physical body to effect the purging of toxins from your system. At this point, it is helpful to assist the purging process by visualizing a spiraling system of Divine Light Vibrations that emanate from your Wulfenite cluster, enter your body at the navel chakra and energize and cleanse organ systems and cellular structures in the abdominal cavity. Hold your Wulfenite in place for fifteen to twenty minutes per Meditation.

5.

When you are ready to terminate your Wulfenite Meditation, slowly count backwards from ten to one. At the count of one, open your eyes and breathe deeply several times. Remain seated or in your reclined position on the floor. Again breathe deeply several times before moving from your Meditation position. For optimum results, it is recommended that the Wulfenite Meditation be performed twice a day for fourteen consecutive days.

II
Discourses

SPIRITUALISM & THE CONSCIENCE OF ONE

The practice of Spiritualism is a way of life that acknowledges, respects and applauds the Light/Life Vibration within all things born of Creation. Spiritualism finds its roots in ancient cultures that flourished more than 200,000 years ago, yet aboriginal cultures such as Native American, African, Asian and native peoples of South America and Australia continue to demonstrate that Spiritualism embodies the grace of coexistence with and the nurturing of the integrity of all the elementals and children of Creation. In the conscience of the Spiritualist, all life forms are sacred - none more, none less than another - each enjoying a blessed function within The God's Divine Order.

Spiritualism teaches that indeed all things upon the face of Mother Earth are mankind's brethren; be it squirrels, trees, flowers, insects or pebbles, all things of Creation contain the same Divine Light Vibration of One. As the most evolved of The God's third density creatures, mankind is charged with the responsibility of bestowing the same Love, Respect, Compassion, Patience and Mercy upon the lesser evolved children of Creation that man would claim as mortal birthright.

The practice of Spiritualism also acknowledges the existence of alternate life forms that coexist with mankind within the third dimension. These alternate life forms or spiritual presences are readily detectable by the initiated Spiritualist, and communication with disembodied beings is commonplace. Many times during the transition phase between incarnations, a soul essence may become trapped intradimensionally. An evolved Spiritualist is able to render assistance to such an Earthbound soul vibration by aiding that soul vibration in breaking its emotional bond with a given place or set of circumstances. It is the release from specific emotional bondage that allows the soul vibration to complete the intradimensional preparations for reincarnation and/or engage ascension to the next level of consciousness.

In a time when "the old ways" *(more simplistic modes of thought and behavior)* are beginning to regain acceptance, many are finding that the value systems inherent to Spiritualism have an immeasurably positive impact upon man's evolving Consciousness of One. In its ability to foster global and Universal resolve for Peace, Love and Compassion, Spiritualism is a beacon forever illuminating the path of Truth and Serenity.

QUARTZ CRYSTAL PROGRAMMING

The concept of programming or infusing Quartz Crystals with specific vibrations, information, emotions and/or desires is one that finds historical basis that predates the advent of modern man. Ancient cultures from Lemuria and Atlantis to Pre-Dynastic Egypt and Mesopotamia to Mayan and Pre-Colombian civilizations utilized Quartz Crystals to store and transmit information, as well as to transmute energy. Alchemists, mystics and other Light-workers of the Post-Christian and Pre-Christian eras programmed several varieties of Quartz Crystals with detailed information regarding the dynamics and nature of Divine Light Vibration and energy transmutation, and many such Crystals are presently being unearthed and accessed for the wealth of information they contain. Also, many Quartz Crystals are found to have perfectly shaped triangles *(known as "records")* etched on one or more apex faces, which indicate that specific information can be accessed by attuning to the vibrations of that Crystal *(See Illustration 6)*.

What are the methods and dynamics of Quartz Crystal Programming? First, it should be noted that Quartz Crystals absorb energy vibrations that run the spectrum from positive to discordant vibrations, and many times a Crystal may carry a number of vibrations, sometimes quite discordant in activity, as a result of having been handled by several different people.

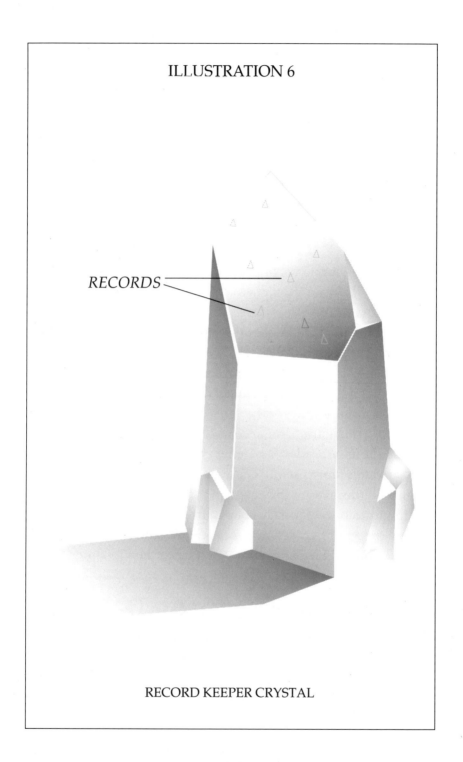

ILLUSTRATION 6

RECORDS

RECORD KEEPER CRYSTAL

Therefore, it is advisable to first cleanse any Crystal that is to be used for programming. *(Crystals used in Meditation as well as programming should first be cleansed and blessed.)*

Cleansing is accomplished by washing the Crystal in cool, running water, followed by placing the Crystal in direct sunlight for an afternoon. Additionally, it is the individual's conscious desire to clear the Crystal of discordant energies during the cleansing process that indeed accomplishes the task. By saying aloud and concentrating on each word, *"I cleanse thee of all discordant vibrations; in The Name of Yahweh, by The Spirit of Christ Jesus, let The Light of The Infinite One radiate within thee"*, purifies and restores the inherent vibration of the Crystal.

The Crystal is now ready for programming. Programming is the act of transferring a conscious thought, emotion or desire, Divine Light Vibration or specific information into the matrix of a Quartz Crystal. Clear Quartz Crystals with cloudy inclusions that terminate in clear apexes are recommended as best for programming. Even though Rose, Amethyst, Citrine, Smoky and other Quartz Crystals can be infused with specific programming, Clear Quartz is suggested as ideal to begin with.

Let us examine specific instances and uses of Programmed Quartz Crystals. Depending upon personal preference, the Crystal to be programmed is either held in the hand or situated at eye level for the individual to gaze upon and into, consciously transmitting energy vibrations that are absorbed by the Crystal.

LOVELIGHT VIBRATIONS

The LoveLight Vibration is Divine Light Energy channeled for the purpose of restoring balance to and/or facilitating well-being of either or both physical and emotional distresses. It is the pristine, cosmic Divine Light Vibration of The One Infinite Creator that when attuned to stimulates sensations and conditions of well-being. As the result of Conviction, Love, Mercy and Compassion, the LoveLight Vibration can be channeled through the heart center, programmed into a Crystal and then given to a person in need of this energy.

When a friend or family member is stricken by illness or injury, a Quartz Crystal can be programmed with the LoveLight Vibration to assist in his or her recovery. The gentle vibrations emitted by such a Crystal will prove most comforting to the debilitated. Also, those suffering grief or depression can benefit greatly from the LoveLight Programmed Crystal. To demonstrate the application of the LoveLight Vibration on a grander scale, large Quartz Crystals can be programmed with an intense amount of the LoveLight Vibration in Group Meditations, then placed in areas of the Planet besieged by war, pollution, starvation, disease and industrial devastation to aid in the transformation of our brethren and Mother Earth.

To program a Crystal with the LoveLight Vibration, select a single terminated, Clear Quartz Crystal Generator with cloudy inclusions, but one that is exceptionally clear at the apex. After cleansing the Crystal, center yourself and focus on the task ahead by breathing deeply, inhaling through the nose and exhaling from the mouth. Continue breathing deeply until you are relaxed and focused.

Now, hold the Crystal before you and begin to gaze upon it. Visualize the situation or person to whom you intend to send the LoveLight Vibration. See the physical characteristics of the situation and/or person in as much detail as possible. Then invoke Divine Guidance by saying, *"Almighty Yahweh, Great Spirit of Light, by The Spirit of Christ Jesus, in Thee do I trust. Fill me with The Light of Thy Presence, Father. Surround me, Father, with Archangel Michael, Archangel Gabriel, Archangel Raphael and Archangel Uriel to assist me in the task ahead."* Then say to yourself, *"Channel The Light of Yah, The LoveLight Vibration of the Universe, to facilitate balance and well-being. Channel The Light of Yah for John or Mary. Channel The Light of Yah. Channel The Light of One."*

As the sensations rise within you, you will experience tingling or chills or a warming, vibratory sensation throughout your body. This is the energy system of your body aligning with the LoveLight Vibration. As the energy begins to swell at your crown and heart centers, consciously direct the vibrations down your arm, into your hand and out through your fingers into the Crystal. Feel the Crystal throb and radiate with the LoveLight Vibration. Then bow your head and say, *"I thank Thee, Father, for Thy gifts and tender mercies."* It is now time to send the Crystal to effect the resolution for which it was programmed. *(See Illustration 7)*

ILLUSTRATION 7

QUARTZ CRYSTAL PROGRAMMING SEQUENCE

It should be noted here that Clear Quartz Crystals that display brilliant rainbow inclusions are particular favorites for the LoveLight Vibration infusion. Crystals that display rainbows of predominantly pink and green are especially good as aids in illness and injury recovery, while Crystals that display rainbows in the blue/purple/gold spectrum are especially good for those who suffer from depression. Crystals that display pink, purple and blue rainbows are particularly helpful in comforting those stricken by grief.

AFFIRMATION REINFORCEMENT

By verbalizing Affirmations and consciously infusing Quartz Crystals with those Affirmations, one is able to produce a resonating energy source that vibrates and intensifies the intentions of the Affirmations. Use four Single Generator Crystals of approximately the same size for this programming.

After cleansing the Crystals, perform the LoveLight Meditation Sequence with the four Crystals situated at the four compass directions with the apexes pointed toward you. After completing the 23rd Psalm, open your eyes and turn to each Crystal. Touch each Crystal with your right hand, gaze upon it and say, *"In The Name of Almighty Yahweh, by The Spirit of Christ Jesus, I beseech Thee to absorb the vibrations of the Affirmations that follow."* Repeat this request three times, then make your sets of Affirmations.

At the conclusion of your LoveLight Meditation, your Crystals will be infused with the vibrations of your Affirmations, and the Tranquility of your Meditation will also have been transferred to your Crystals. Place one of your Programmed Crystals under your pillow or at your bedside, so that the vibrations of your Affirmations will be near you while you sleep. Place another Crystal in your car and one in your desk at work, or carry one in your pocket or purse. Every time you see or touch one of your Programmed Crystals you will be reminded of your Affirmations by the energy transmitted to you from the Crystal. These Crystals will quickly become a source of great comfort, inspiration and joy, for you will want to handle them more and more as your Affirmations become realized. *(See Illustration 8)*

ILLUSTRATION 8

AFFIRMATION REINFORCEMENT

ANGER AND FEAR
TRANSFERENCE AND TRANSMUTATION

When situations arise that evoke moods of great anger or intense fear, programming a Quartz Crystal with the emotions can result in the transmutation of the fears and angers that are counterproductive and often debilitating.

Select a Clear Quartz Crystal of one to two inches in length with an abundance of cloudy inclusions in its shaft, but that culminates in a virtually clear point. Sit with the Crystal in a quiet room and visualize the situation that caused the fear or anger response. Speak to the Crystal and say, *"In The Name of Yahweh, by The Spirit of Christ Jesus, I humbly ask that my fears (angers) are transferred to the body of this Crystal."* Then isolate the people involved in your fear or anger scenario. Visualize the details of the faces and physiques. Again speak to the Crystal and say, *"I place my anger toward Jim or Mary within the body of this Crystal,"* or *"I place my fear of Mary or Jim within the body of this Crystal."*

Feel the discordant emotions leave you, as the Crystal begins to warm and begins pulsating in your hand. Then place the Crystal in direct sunlight and gaze upon it. Think of the sunlight bathing the Crystal and your discordant vibrations it contains

259

with glowing, radiant, transformational energy. Think of your fear or anger swirling around in the cloudy inclusions of the Crystal, eager to break free into the clarity of the apex and be kissed by the benevolent sunlight. Watch as your discordant energy is cleansed and transformed, as it leaves this dimension through the glistening apex of the Crystal. Know that now you can face similar situations without reacting with fear or with anger. *(See Illustration 9)*

If however, the fear or anger sensations begin to return, simply visualize the sunlight bathing your Crystal and the discordant emotions it contained with warm, penetrating, Loving rays of Golden/White Light. Visualize your discordant emotions as they travel from the Crystal unto the ether, and are permanently transmuted into vibrations of Peace and Love.

Another technique of fear and anger transmutation is to take a Crystal that has been programmed with your fear and/or anger to a large body of water near a wooded area. Invoke the devic spirits of the forest and turn to the four compass directions and call upon Archangelic Presence to assist you in ridding yourself of discordant emotions. Then cast the Crystal into the water, and visualize your fears and angers leaving you to be washed clean by the flowing waters. Should your inappropriate feelings recur, simply again visualize yourself casting the Crystal into the waters to be cleansed of discordant emotions. Each time you make this visualization your discordant vibrations will become less and less charged, until your discordant energy is totally transformed into vibrations of Peace and Love. *(See Illustration 10)*

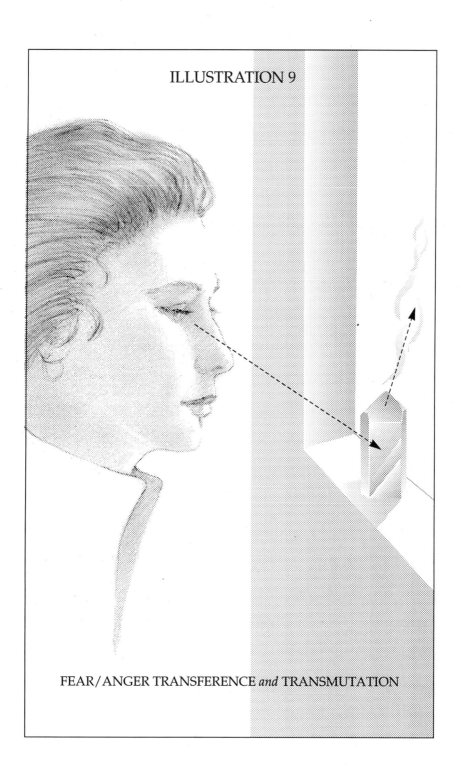

ILLUSTRATION 9

FEAR/ANGER TRANSFERENCE *and* TRANSMUTATION

ILLUSTRATION 10

FEAR/ANGER TRANSFERENCE *and* TRANSMUTATION
with QUARTZ CRYSTAL *and* WATER

TELEPATHIC COMMUNICATION

When two people or a group of people are of like mind and purpose, that is when two people or a group of people are motivated by Light-minded intentions, then telepathic communication can be engaged through the use of Programmed Quartz Crystals. Telepathic communication is successfully performed by persons who have developed their skills of focusing, visualizing and channeling directed information and/or energy, skills that are accessible to and can be developed by most. Programmed Quartz Crystals serve as amplification tools in the transmission and reception processes.

Many times when communications are transmitted, varying time spans are required for the conscious mind to acknowledge and assimilate the transmitted information. Many times, the conscious mind is totally unaware that the ethereal self, the soul essence, the subconscious mind has received and processed any information at all. However, it is the directive of the intuitive soul to integrate Light-minded information into the matrix of the human consciousness for expression in the Earth Plane. Therefore, transmitted information will continue to seek expression in the physical plane within the proper time/space sequence of Soul Evolution, until the appropriate expression has been achieved. What is addressed here is the motivation of the soul to transmute the ego with Light-minded vibrations to enable the total being to emerge as a soul initiate, a being who has assimilated The Truths of Existence and who has found Oneness in the heart of Creation. What this last statement implies is that the effectiveness of telepathic communications are directly dependent upon individual readiness, which acknowledges the stage of Soul Evolution that would allow the reception and application of telepathic information in the physical plane.

Clear Quartz Crystals of specific apex geometry are recommended for use in telepathic communication programming. Crystals with alternating seven and three-sided faces of perfect symmetry have proven to be the most effective transmitting and receiving Crystals. The exception to this statement, however, is the group of double terminated Tabular Clear Quartz Crystals that will be discussed later. Clear Quartz Crystals of perfect symmetry with alternating seven and three-sided faces embody the harmonious balance of Oneness. By programming these Crystals with specific information, transmission is accomplished by one's conscious desire to initiate said transmission. Of course, the person to whom transmission is sent should also have a Crystal of specific geometry to aid in the reception of transmitted information. *(See Illustration 11)*

After cleansing your Crystal, center and focus your attention on the information to be transmitted. Hold your crystal and begin to gaze upon it, concentrating your efforts upon the lower half of the Crystal's shaft into the area of cloudy inclusions. After a time, place the largest of the seven-sided faces against your forehead at the third eye center. Mentally focus upon and recite the information you desire to transmit. Then hold the Crystal with the apex pointed away from your body and say,

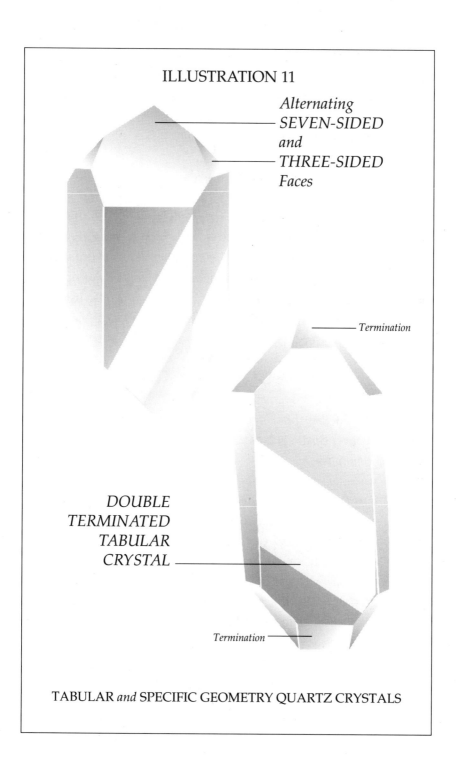

ILLUSTRATION 11

Alternating
SEVEN-SIDED
and
THREE-SIDED
Faces

Termination

DOUBLE
TERMINATED
TABULAR
CRYSTAL

Termination

TABULAR *and* SPECIFIC GEOMETRY QUARTZ CRYSTALS

"Transmit". You will notice an energy surge in your body as the information is dispatched. When the transmission has been completed and reception acknowledged, cleanse your Crystal by washing it in cool, running water and placing it in direct sunlight. *(See Illustration 12)*

Reception of the transmitted information is accomplished in a similar fashion. As the information is being transmitted, the etheric self of the intended recipient is impacted upon by the transmission. Through the intuitive process, the conscious mind becomes aware of the intended transmission. At this point, depending upon the recipient's skills and stage of development, the information is either consciously channeled by the intended recipient or a Crystal of specific geometry is used to assist. If the Crystal is used, the largest of the seven-sided faces is placed against the forehead at the third eye center to amplify the transmission. Once the information is received, the recipient would simply say, *"Transmission received"*, while holding the Crystal against the third eye center. Then the Crystal is held with the apex pointing away from the body and the request, *"Transmit"*, is made.

Double terminated Tabular Quartz Crystals are also excellent tools for use in telepathic communications. Tabular Quartz Crystals are Clear Quartz Crystals that have two opposing sides that are wider than the other remaining four sides, which gives these Crystals a characteristic "ring" that indicates that Tabular Quartz Crystals vibrate at a much higher rate than other Clear Quartz Crystals. The double termination feature of some Tabular Crystals identifies these Clear Quartz Crystals as having two perfectly formed termination points at both ends of the Crystals. The double termination feature allows for simultaneous transmission and reception of information, as vibrations travel in both directions through the termination

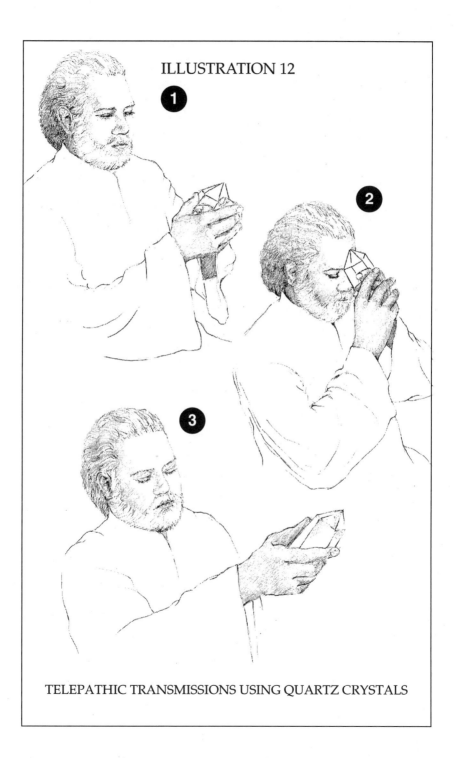

ILLUSTRATION 12

TELEPATHIC TRANSMISSIONS USING QUARTZ CRYSTALS

points of double terminated Tabular Quartz Crystals. It should be stated here that double terminated Tabular Crystals that are suitable for telepathic communications are not commonplace, and when they are encountered, these Crystals usually command rather high premiums.

To effect communication, double terminated Tabular Quartz Crystals do not require programming. After cleansing the Crystal, center yourself and focus on the information to be transmitted. Hold the Crystal in your right hand with one apex pointed toward you and the other termination pointed away from you. Gaze upon the Crystal and concentrate on the information you wish to transmit. Visualize the person, in detail, for whom the information is intended. See the bone structure and features of the person's face, the eyes, nose, mouth, teeth, chin, ears and hair. The Tabular Crystal will begin to vibrate and become warm. Now, mentally project the information you wish to send and say, "Transmit". The information projected will be dispatched and confirmation will be received instantaneously, as the energy systems of your body surge with Divine Light Vibrations.

SPIRIT GUIDES AND ASCENDED TEACHERS

Each soul incarnate has and can identify the presence of Spirit Guides and Ascended Teachers, whose function is to aid the soul incarnate in negotiating the elements of consciousness. Frequently, Spirit Guides are entities who have coexisted with the soul incarnate in prior incarnations and who project "road signs" that alert the soul incarnate to potential pitfalls and counterproductive behavior patterns. The "road signs" projected by Spirit Guides may appear in a number of forms such as:

1 - a clear vision of a course of behavior that would lead to either a fruitful or undesirable outcome.
2 - a vision of similar situations superimposed one upon the other to illustrate behavior patterns and typical results.
3 - a visual appearance of a Spirit Guide (*usually during Meditation*) either smiling in agreement with a considered course of action or discouraging the considered course by shaking its head in disapproval.
4 - the appearance of a Spirit Guide and the transmission of clues in the Spirit Guide's facial expressions and/or body language as well as color impressions surrounding the Spirit Guide.

5 - audibly channeled information that points out potential
hardships or successes resultant from the soul incarnate's
choices of goal directions, behaviors and associations.

*(It should be noted that one's intuitive self can also be responsible for
projecting "road signs". However, as a function of Spiritual
Attunement, the individual learns to differentiate between the
influence of Spirit Guides and the intuitive self.)*

Ascended Teachers serve as messengers of Universal Law and
Divine Will, offering both visual and verbal references designed
to instruct the soul incarnate and enable him/her to comprehend
the dynamics and Wisdom of The Lessons of Existence.

One Visualization/Meditation technique that allows one to
identify his/her Spirit Guides and Ascended Teachers is as
follows:

1.

Select a palm-size Clear Quartz Generator Point that you have
cleansed and blessed and seat yourself in an upright position in
a quiet, dimly lit room. Begin to relax yourself by breathing in
deeply through the nose and exhaling from the mouth . As you
inhale, visualize glowing, transformational Golden/White Light
Energy entering through your nostrils, filling your chest and
heart center. As you exhale, visualize all tension, frustration and
disharmony leaving you in dark, cloudy energy swirls that you
expel from your mouth. Bless yourself and your discordant
energy in The Name of Yahweh, by The Spirit of Christ Jesus, as
you cast this dissonant energy unto the ether to find Peace.
Breathe deeply several times until you have become relaxed.

2.

Pick up your Crystal and hold it in your left palm. Place your right hand beneath your left and cradle your Crystal in your lap. Bow your head and begin to gaze upon your Crystal. Project your consciousness into the Crystal and become one with the Crystal. Become the walls of your Crystal. Look up to the apex, then down to the base. Feel the vibrations of Divine Light Energy passing through you. Float within the swirls and inclusions of your Crystal. Now, find a quiet, clear place within the Crystal and settle there.

3.

In the quiet, clear place that you have found within the Crystal, begin to visualize a favorite place in nature that you have visited or have dreamed of visiting. It may be an ocean setting where the waves are gently rising to caress the sands, with sea gulls hovering overhead, or a bubbling brook trickling through a forest while squirrels scamper up the sides of a tree, or a mountain setting where the air is so sweet you can taste it - any setting in nature where you might feel at Peace and One with Creation. Once you have visualized this wonderfully nurturing place, see yourself in the midst of the splendor of your nature setting, feeling secure and comforted by the sights, sounds and aromas of Mother Earth.

4.

Now that you have become fully integrated with your serene setting, simply say, *"I call upon my Spirit Guides and Ascended Teachers to join me in my mountain paradise"* (or ocean, woodland, desert oasis, etc.). Relax and continue to absorb the sights, sounds and aromas of your paradise. After a time, additional images will appear. Your Spirit Guides and Ascended Teachers will come forth and allow themselves to be seen. One or more images will develop and you will intuitively know that you are communing with Spirit Guides and/or Ascended Teachers. *(See Illustration 13)*

5.

In The Name of Yahweh, thank the Spirit(s) for revealing him/herself to you and ask by what name the Spirit is called. The Spirit will willingly answer and more often than not you will register sensations within your chakra system that you will learn to associate with Spirit presence. Converse with the Spirit for as long as the vision remains and before returning to the reality of your Mediation room, again thank the Spirit in the name of Yahweh for revealing him/herself to you. From this time forth you will have the ability to call upon your Spirit Guides and/or Ascended Teachers by name when you feel the need for communing with them, and you will also enjoy unexpected appearances by your Spirit Guides and Ascended Teachers as situations so warrant.

NOTE: If after several attempts to contact your Spirit Guides and Ascended Teachers you are unsuccessful, do not give up. Not everyone is successful on the first or second attempt. Be patient and diligent, as your efforts will ultimately be successful.

Another Visualization/Meditation technique used to access Spirit Guides and Ascended Teachers utilizes Clear Quartz Clusters. Select a Clear Quartz Cluster that gives you the feeling that the cluster resembles a Crystal City. Allow your intuition to guide you in your selection. After you have relaxed yourself in an appropriate Meditation setting, begin to gaze upon and merge with the Crystal Cluster. Look upon each Crystal in the

ILLUSTRATION 13

ACCESSING SPIRIT GUIDES *and* ASCENDED TEACHERS

cluster as a separate Crystal Building within the Crystal City. Allow yourself to enter and explore each building in the city. There will be one Crystal Building within the Crystal City that you will be especially drawn to enter. It will be within this Crystal Building that your Spirit Guides and/or Ascended Teachers will make their existence known.

Upon entering this Crystal Building, allow yourself to wander through the halls until you come upon a comfortable, familiar room, a room decorated in a manner that is warm and nurturing to your senses. This room may contain familiar objects and/or aromas, or may be filled with objects from your dreams. Frequently, there will be a glowing light that emanates from outside the room that illuminates the room in a soft, welcoming manner.

Seat yourself within your Crystal Room and ask that your Spirit Guides and Ascended Teachers join you. Relax and after a time one or more Spirits will appear and allow their purposes to be known. Do not forget to thank your Spirit Guides and Ascended Teachers in The Name of Yahweh for granting you communion with them, and for assisting you in your evolutionary journey.

NOTE: When communing with Spirits and/or receiving channeled information, it is strongly recommended that you identify the Spirit presence by asking its name, asking by what authority the Spirit communes with you and finally by asking the Spirit to call the name of God (The Infinite One, Yahweh, Jehovah, Allah, Brahma, etc.). If the Spirit Presence is in any way illusive, vague, uncooperative, demanding or manipulative or should you feel in any way uncomfortable with the energy transmission, it is suggested that you simply thank the Spirit for the time of communion, bless it with Love in The Light of One and ask it to return to its place of birth to find Peaceful resolution.

INVOCATION OF THE ARCHANGELS

In the practice of Spiritualism, Divine Presence is commonly invoked to assist soul incarnates and Initiates of The Light of One in negotiating third dimension realities. Though we can call upon literally hundreds of forms of The God Presence to satisfy requirements for different times, places, conditions and needs, Archangelic Vibrations are most often called upon to provide guidance and blessing. Archangelic Presence is The Divine Light Vibration of a specific element of The God Spirit (not a personified, tangible being) invoked to facilitate and/or to provide guidance in the execution of a specific Earthly task. The nature of Archangel Vibrations varies with need and purpose, as each Archangel's energy matrix can be readily identified and invoked by name. For purposes of Meditation and for many ceremonies and rituals, four Archangels are primarily invoked as messengers of The God Spirit. These Archangels are Michael, Gabriel, Raphael and Uriel. In addition to these four Archangels, three other Archangelic Vibrations will be briefly discussed later.

Archangel Michael is designated as the Archangelic Presence that is like unto God, The All-Knowing Presence, possessing dominion over all discordant energies, and is invoked from the east, the direction that symbolizes knowledge and enlightenment. Archangel Michael is associated with the purple

.ay in the Spectrum of Divine Light Vibrations as found in the deep purple of Amethyst, and is acknowledged as the highest, most evolved energy matrix of the Angelic Order.

Archangel Gabriel is designated as the Divine Presence that is The Strength and Conviction of God, and is invoked from the west, the direction from which many cultures acknowledge that danger and disharmony arise. Archangel Gabriel is associated with the yellow/gold ray in the Spectrum of Divine Light Vibrations as amplified through Golden Topaz and/or Golden Citrine.

Archangel Raphael is designated as the Archangelic Presence that facilitates physical and emotional well-being through The God Spirit, and is invoked from the north, the direction that symbolizes life. Archangel Raphael is associated with the green ray of The Divine Light Spectrum that is seen in the rich shades of Elbaite (Green Tourmaline), and functions to transform the emotional pain and karmic wounds of mankind as the children of Creation endeavor to learn The Lessons of Existence.

Archangel Uriel is designated as the Archangel of the sage, the Archangelic Vibration that is The Light of God, illuminating the path of the soul initiate with The Wisdom of One, and is invoked from the south, the direction that expresses the resolution of Peace and quiet. Archangel Uriel is associated with the dark blue ray in The Divine Light Spectrum as found in the deep, rich blue of Lapis Lazuli.

1.

The LoveLight Prayer/Invocation given in this text is most effective in invoking the energy presence of the Archangels. To prepare for your Invocation, select a Clear Quartz Generator of specific apex geometry that has alternating faces of seven sides and three sides. If such a Crystal is not available and indeed these Crystals of specific apex geometry are not commonplace, then select the most dynamic Clear Quartz Generator in your Crystal collection to serve as your amplification tool for this Invocation.

2.

Invocation of the Archangels can be performed indoors in a room in which you usually engage in Meditation, or in an outdoor setting, a place in which you feel especially close to Mother Earth, a place in which you feel The Oneness of Creation. After cleansing and blessing your Crystal, cradle the Crystal in your hands, right hand beneath the left, with the apex pointing up and away from your body. Now, stand facing the east and proclaim your Allegiance to The Universal One by saying, *"Almighty Yah, Great Spirit of Light, by The Spirit of Christ Jesus, in Thee do I trust."* Next, begin your Invocation by calling upon the energy presence of Archangel Michael, asking that you be granted communion with the Archangelic Presence that is like unto God. Turn clockwise now to face the west and call upon Archangel Gabriel for strength and conviction. Again turn clockwise to face the north and call upon Archangel Raphael, asking that facilitating vibrations join with you. Now, turn counterclockwise, retracing your steps, to face the south and call upon the energy presence of Archangel Uriel for guidance in your journey toward enlightenment. *(As you invoke the energies of the different Archangels, visualize the color associated with each Archangel.)* Now, turn counterclockwise one final time to again face the east.

3.

Next, while holding the Crystal in both hands, place the largest of the seven sided faces against your third eye. If the Crystal that you have chosen for this Invocation is not one of specific apex geometry, then place the largest of the six faces against your third eye. Hold the Crystal in place for one to three minutes. Very quickly you may begin to experience visionary sequences and energy movements from head to toe. Allow yourself to merge and commune with The Divine Light Vibrations that you have invoked, as you will know on either or both an intuitive and a conscious level that you have been touched by messengers of The God Spirit. *(Illustrations 14 through 16 outline the procedure for invoking the combined Divine Light Vibration of the four Archangels.)*

An alternate method for invoking Archangelic Presence can be performed in a stationary position with the eyes closed. After engaging a rhythmic, deep breathing sequence and offering your Prayer of Allegiance, begin your Invocation by peering upward through the third eye center to invoke Archangel Michael. Next, look downward to invoke Archangel Gabriel. Now, turn your eyes to the left to invoke Archangel Raphael. Finally, look down and back across to the far right to complete the Invocation with Archangel Uriel. Complete the sequence three times, using the words, *"In The Name of Yahweh, by The Spirit of Christ Jesus, I invoke The Presence of Archangel Michael to join with me this day."* Then speak the same words silently to invoke Archangel Gabriel, Archangel Raphael and Archangel Uriel. This procedure can be incorporated in your daily Meditation practices to help infuse your consciousness with conviction and guidance through Divine Light Vibrations.

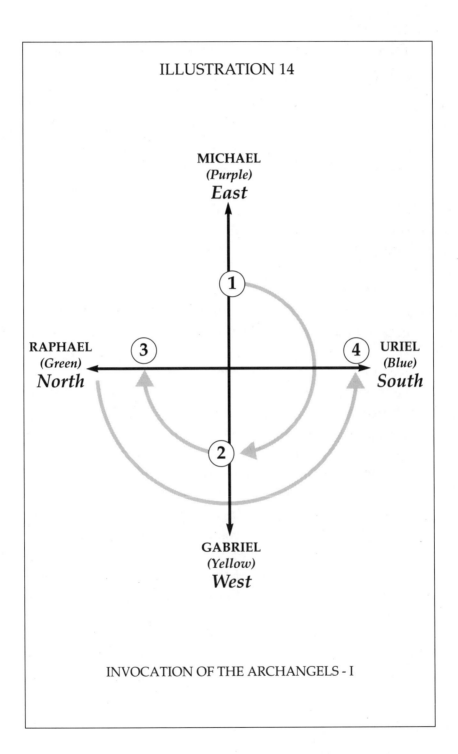

ILLUSTRATION 14

MICHAEL
(Purple)
East

RAPHAEL
(Green)
North

URIEL
(Blue)
South

GABRIEL
(Yellow)
West

INVOCATION OF THE ARCHANGELS - I

Three additional Archangelic Energies, Archangels Barachiel, Jehudial and Salatiel, are commonly invoked in association with Archangels Michael, Gabriel, Raphael and Uriel. Archangel Barachiel embodies The Divine Light Vibration that is The Blessing of God, Archangel Jehudial, The Divine Light Vibration that is The Praise of God and Archangel Salatiel, The Divine Light Vibration that is The Prayer of God. These three Divine Light Vibrations exist within the energy matrix of the Invocation of Archangels Michael, Gabriel, Raphael and Uriel and correspond respectively to the designations or directions, "Above, Below and Within." *(Further, within the energy patterns of each of the four major Archangelic Vibrations lie several levels or communication states that are Angelic forms who can be invoked and/or dispatched as messengers, guardians, guides or representations of The Living God Spirit.)*

In all that is done in the practice of Spiritualism, probably one of the most fulfilling and illuminating experiences involve the Invocation of Archangelic Presence, for it is the nurturing, cleansing, inspiring vibration of The Living God Spirit that is communed with and instilled in one's consciousness during such an Invocation. It is the infusion of Light-minded energy into the nature of one's being and the awakening of dormant memories of the expression of Absolute Truth that are accomplished by invoking the energy of the Archangels. And by accessing the Living, Loving vibration of the Archangels, mankind can learn *(that is, relearn)* to embrace and intimately comprehend the nature of The Spirit of God alive within the soul of mortal man.

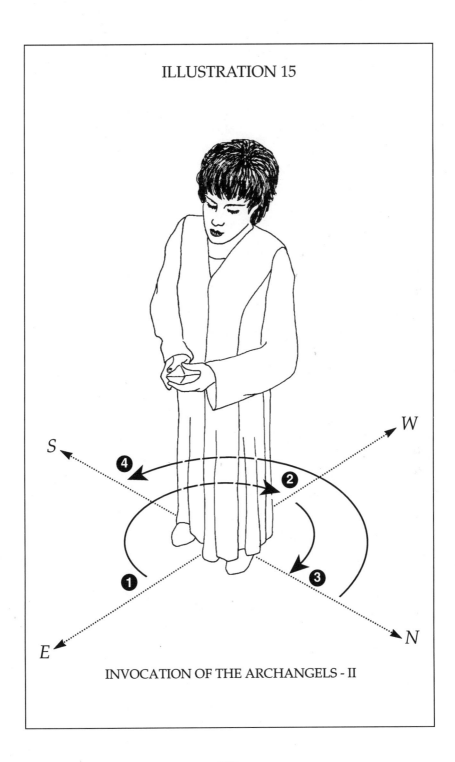

ILLUSTRATION 15

INVOCATION OF THE ARCHANGELS - II

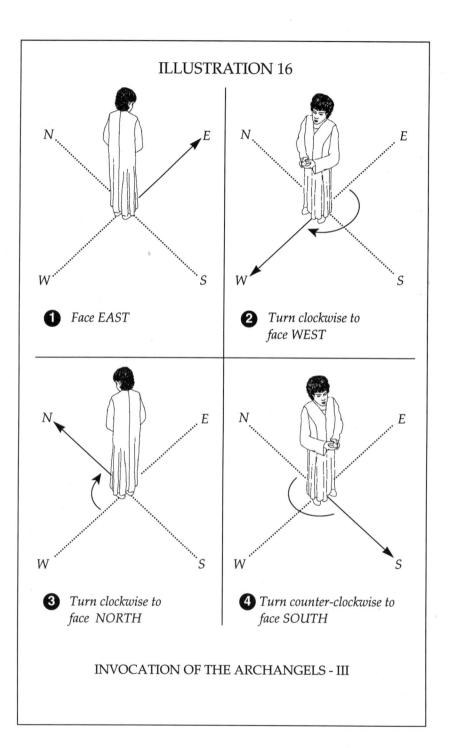

ILLUSTRATION 16

❶ *Face EAST*

❷ *Turn clockwise to face WEST*

❸ *Turn clockwise to face NORTH*

❹ *Turn counter-clockwise to face SOUTH*

INVOCATION OF THE ARCHANGELS - III

CHAKRA SYSTEM DYNAMICS

The chakra system is responsible for the balance and flow of Divine Light Vibrations *(electrical energy transmissions)* throughout the physical and auric bodies that stimulate, regulate and nurture all bodily functions and states of consciousness. Simply put, chakras are energy centers or "wheels of light" that exist above, within and penetrate through the physical body, and are responsible for the regulation and movement of Divine Light Vibrations that impact upon and translate into both general and specific states of physical, emotional and spiritual well-being or conditions of distress. Frequently, by scanning or observing the orientation or the type and degree of closure, blockage or openness of a particular chakra, inferences can be drawn concerning the relative state of physical health of the corresponding body region. *(Techniques for scanning chakra conditions involve highly sensitive intuitive abilities, as well as specialized skills in the detection of subtle energy fields.)* Additionally, the relative efficiency of the immune system *(gland)* that corresponds to each chakra can be analyzed and assessed as a function of the general state of that specific chakra, thereby affording medical technology yet another diagnostic tool in the wholistic treatment of the human organism. *Illustration 17* shows the placement of the primary and meridian chakras of the body and lists the corresponding glands of the immune system.

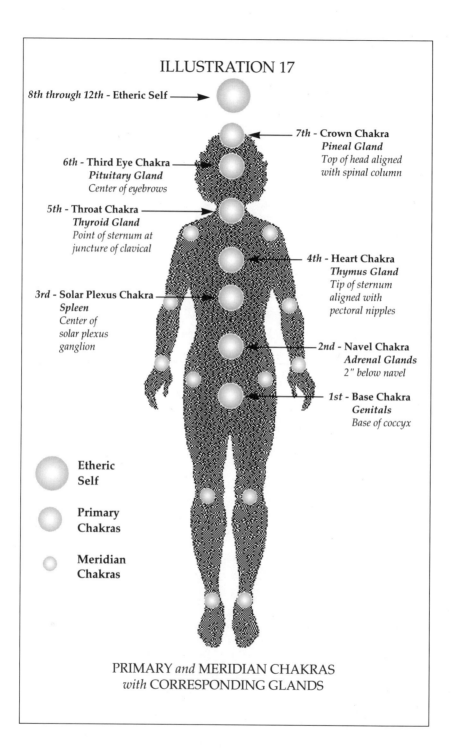

ILLUSTRATION 17

8th through 12th - Etheric Self ──▶

7th - **Crown Chakra**
Pineal Gland
Top of head aligned
with spinal column

*6th - * **Third Eye Chakra**
Pituitary Gland
Center of eyebrows

*5th - * **Throat Chakra**
Thyroid Gland
Point of sternum at
juncture of clavical

4th - **Heart Chakra**
Thymus Gland
Tip of sternum
aligned with
pectoral nipples

*3rd - * **Solar Plexus Chakra**
Spleen
Center of
solar plexus
ganglion

2nd - **Navel Chakra**
Adrenal Glands
2" below navel

1st - **Base Chakra**
Genitals
Base of coccyx

**Etheric
Self**

**Primary
Chakras**

**Meridian
Chakras**

PRIMARY *and* MERIDIAN CHAKRAS
with CORRESPONDING GLANDS

CHART IV
Crystal/Mineral - Chakra Associations

BASE CHAKRA - 1st

Apache Tears
Black Tourmaline *(Schorl)*
Fire Agate
Garnet
Hematite
Mahogany Obsidian
Neptunite

Plume Agate
Rainbow Obsidian
Rhodonite
Ruby
Snowflake Obsidian
Smoky Quartz
Tourmalated Quartz

NAVEL CHAKRA - 2nd

Amber
Barite
Bloodstone
Carnelian
Chrysotile
Citrine Quartz
Fire Agate
Mahogany
Moss Agate

Plume Agate
Pyrophyllite
Realgar
Rutilated Quartz
Tiger's Eye
Topaz *(Imperial, Golden)*
Vanadanite
Wulfenite

SOLAR PLEXUS CHAKRA - 3rd

Amber
Apatite *(Yellow)*
Chrysotile
Malachite
Pampa Onyx

Peridot
Rhodocrosite
Sulfur
Sunstone
Topaz *(Golden)*

HEART CHAKRA - 4th

Actinolite
Alunite
Atacamite
Aventurine *(Green)*
Chrysocolla
Chrysoprase
Chrysotile
Cuprite
Dioptase
Emerald
Green Tourmaline *(Elbaite)*
Jade

Kunzite *(Pink)*
Moonstone
Orthoclase
Pampa Onyx
Peridot
Pink Tourmaline
Rhodocrosite
Rose Quartz
Unakite
Variscite
Zoisite

THROAT CHAKRA - 5th

Amazonite
Apatite *(Blue)*
Aquamarine
Blue lace Agate
Blue Tourmaline *(Indicolite)*

Kyanite *(Blue)*
Larimar
Turquoise
Youngite

THIRD EYE CHAKRA - 6th

Amethyst
Apophyllite
Azurite
Calcite
Chalcopyrite
Fluorite
Iolite
Labradorite

Lapis Lazuli
Lazulite
Moonstone
Pyrite
Smithsonite
Sodalite
Sugilite
Youngite

CROWN CHAKRA - 7th

Adamite

Apophyllite

Aragonite

Calcite

Celestite

Clear Quartz

Danberite

Diamond

Moonstone

Satin Kyanite

Selenite

Ulexite

ETHERIC SELF - 8TH *through* 12th

Adamite

Anhydrite

Apophyllite

Calcite *(Mango, Salmon)*

Onyx

Smithsonite

Stibnite

Zebrastone

Chart IV lists the primary Crystals and Minerals that influence or activate the various chakras.

In discussing the nature of human energy systems, it should be acknowledged that active systems of memories and patterns of behaviors evolve through present as well as successive past incarnations that influence the predisposition for particular energy states displayed by the various chakras during the present incarnation. Further, it should also be noted that the existence of either specific higher or lower consciousness phases bear direct correlation to chakra states and translate into specific, identifiable thought and behavior tendencies. Chart V-1 and Chart V-2 list the behavior tendencies associated with each chakra that are attributable to either higher or lower consciousness phases.

In acknowledging memory systems, patterns of behavior and consciousness phases, it is equally as important to identify existing chakra orientations* that will clearly indicate the nature or phase of energy/behavior tendency that can be expected. For instance, if we observe that an individual's navel chakra is blocked by discordant energy and upon further examination of the navel area by scanning, we discover that the navel chakra is partially or fully closed as well, then we can deduce that the individual's ability to implement behaviors of Godliness will be severely compromised, indicating the existence of a lower energy phase. In all probability, this will be a soul incarnate with a myriad of unresolved conflicts that he/she will have literally "swallowed" and repressed, but nevertheless remains unconsciously impacted by in many aspects of life. It is the

* For detailed explanation of chakra orientations, see pages 229-234 of *"Discussions of Spiritual Attunement & Soul Evolution, Volume II"* by Sri Akhenaton.

direct result of unresolved emotional conflicts that we observe reactionary behaviors, defensive attitudes, denials of emotional realities and a reluctance to "let go" of counterproductive, established patterns of thought and behavior.

Conversely, should we find an individual's navel chakra to be open, resilient and generating a warm, unrestricted flow of energy, then we can deduce that the individual's expression of self will tend to be benevolent, out-going, generous, Loving and characterized by behaviors that indicate states of God-Conscious Being are the acknowledged reality of the individual. This will tend to be the profile of a soul incarnate whose choices in life are made with the clear intent of directly affecting The Greater Good for all Creation, instead of focusing upon the single-minded drives and the compelling, coercing impulses of the ego-self. With this in mind, we can conclude that this individual's behavior is guided by higher, more evolved phases of consciousness that will ultimately lead this child of God to the moment of conscious ascension into The Infinite Body of God.

Dysfunctional chakra dynamics that result from discordant memory systems and the maintenance of lower consciousness phases are further influenced by fears, hostilities and judgemental, reactionary behavior patterns that serve to perpetuate discordant behaviors that in turn impede the development of Light-minded Consciousness and the evolution of the God-self. However, through the process of Healing Facilitation, discordant energy matrices can be identified in mortal consciousness and can subsequently be transformed. Through this process of transformation, dysfunctional energies from haunting memories and unresolved emotional conflicts are surfaced and released, allowing the soul incarnate to embrace, understand and accept the nature and dynamics of his/her past, counterproductive thought and behavior patterns. It is at this

CHART V - 1

CHAKRA STATES & ASSOCIATED BEHAVIORS

LOWER, EGOCENTRIC PHASE

1st (Base) Chakra: Establishment and Maintenance of Personal Survival Drives and Personal Embellishments

2nd (Navel) Chakra: Control of Physical Reality through Conquest, Manipulation, Acquisition, Accomplishment, Dominance, Self-importance

3rd (Solar Plexus) Chakra: Execution of Personal Will and Impact of Emotional Matrix upon Attitudes and Behaviors

4th (Heart) Chakra: Behaviors Motivated by Drives of Self-worth and Need for Protection of Illusions of Ego-self

5th (Throat) Chakra: Repression of Personal Reality of Truth

6th (Third Eye) Chakra: Analysis, Speculation and Logical Progressions of Linear Thought Process; Rationalization and Justification for Self-serving Behaviors

7th (Crown) Chakra: Rejection of Spiritual Path as Viable or Practical Life-plan

CHART V - 2

CHAKRA STATES & ASSOCIATED BEHAVIORS

HIGHER, GOD-CONSCIOUS PHASE

1st (Base) Chakra: Cooperation

2nd (Navel) Chakra: Implementation of Godliness in Daily Behavior

3rd (Solar Plexus) Chakra: Selflessness

4th (Heart) Chakra: Expressions of God-self

5th (Throat) Chakra: Verbalizations of Divine Truth

6th (Third Eye) Chakra: Evolved Perceptions of Reality; Perceptions of Truth in The Light of One

7th (Crown) Chakra: Realization of Divine Consciousness

8th through 12th Chakras: Elements of Higher Self
(Etheric Consciousness States that seek to integrate with the conscious thought process to develop Light-minded behavior)

point that the soul incarnate can consciously choose to develop a more evolved, heart-centered pattern of behavior, for the evolution of consciousness and the transformation of egocentric drives are vital in the conscious engagement of the path toward enlightenment - as through heart-centered behavior shines The Light and The Wisdom of The One.

CHAKRA SEALING AND THE COUNCIL OF TWELVE

At this time in human development, many soul incarnates are becoming aware of the energy systems that surround, penetrate and influence every aspect of mortal existence. Many are and have been aware of tingling sensations, chills or flashes of heat surging along their spinal columns and have been at a loss to explain such experiences. Indeed the nature of the chakra system is a mystery to most, as formal education (particularly in western society) has not prepared mortal man to comprehend the dynamics of the energy systems of the human body. Nevertheless, many soul incarnates have experienced these "unusual sensations" since early childhood.

As each individual soul vibration encounters the elements of his/her journey, it becomes necessary to make decisions that impact upon the course of that individual's evolutionary path. When the moment arrives that makes it mandatory to investigate the nature of the energy systems of the Universe, the soul incarnate opens the door to accepting the Ethereal Consciousness that is beyond the realm of occidental traditions.

As each soul incarnate evolves and finds him/herself assimilating higher levels of consciousness, the moment approaches when the chakra system of the incarnate soul is energized, balanced and sealed by Divine Light Vibrations of the

Universe. The process of chakra sealing is that of initiation and acknowledgement that the soul incarnate has evolved to the understanding and conscious application of Universal Law upon the Earth Plane. This does not mean that the individual is now deemed a "perfect being" by the Elders of the Universe; rather, that the soul incarnate has chosen to transmute the ego *(and in large part has successfully done so)* to enable the soul incarnate to serve the needs of mankind as an Initiate of The Light of The Universal One.

Chakra sealing initiates a series of physical, emotional, spiritual and conceptual changes within the energy matrix of the individual that facilitates the integration of Divine Will through man's choice of behavior upon the Earth Plane. At the instant of sealing, the seven primary chakras are opened, energized, balanced and sealed so that the energy systems of the initiate vibrate at the same rate, harmonizing with Universal Light Vibrations. Chakra sealing also amplifies the soul initiate's conscious and intuitive channeling processes, as well as intensifies visionary abilities through cosmic illumination.

The Elders, the evolved Divine Light Vibrations known as The Council of Twelve, provide chakra seals for mortal incarnates to enable man to better comprehend the nature of mankind's Light-minded being, and to enhance each initiate's ability to share the consciousness of Divine Light with the children of Creation. The Council of Twelve is a group of individual, highly evolved social memory complexes, each one distinct and complete unto itself, yet in perfect harmony with the eleven others. Envoys from The Council were dispatched to Lemuria and Atlantis thousands of years ago, where They temporarily took physical form and were then known as The Oversouls. Absolute clarity of Galactic Order in Divine Light Vibration transmission is the function of The Council of Twelve, as These are They who fashioned the galactic plan for Earth. The Yahweh Entity, The Creator of modern man, is one member of The Council of Twelve. The Council embodies the consciousness of The Infinite One, and is responsible for bonding the sacred covenant of LoveLight Vibration. *(It should be noted that some fully sealed Initiates of The Light of One, such as the author of this text, are authorized by The Council of Twelve to perform the sealing of one, two or three chakras for those soul incarnates who are ready and willing to accept this step in evolution. And on rare occasions, the sealing of the first seven primary chakras is authorized. However, let it be clearly understood that only by direct sanction and guidance of The Council of Twelve can any Initiate conscionably engage in the administering of chakra seals.)*

The Council of Twelve benevolently assists any soul incarnate who chooses to accept The Wisdom and Conscience of One in his/her evolutionary journey. This Body of Intergalactic Truth is One with all things - therefore, all that mankind thinks and does, has thought and has done, will think and will do lives within the conscious memory and thoughts of The Council of Twelve. It is the purpose of The Council to receive those soul incarnates who endeavor to uphold the precepts of Universal Law, and who understand that by serving the needs of mankind and Mother Earth, in whatever manner one might choose or be directed, we as soul initiates are indeed serving the purpose of The Greater Good of all Creation.

III

Crystal & Mineral Properties

The list that follows outlines the primary characteristics of Crystals and Minerals as determined by our study, practical applications and through channeled information received at Portal Enterprises. Bear in mind, however, that the properties listed below need not be the only properties that can be ascribed to a given Crystal or Mineral. Therefore, we suggest that the information given below be used as the foundation upon which you allow your intuition and experience to build your personal knowledge of Crystal and Mineral properties.

ACTINOLITE: increases energy matrix capacity through the expansion and reinforcement of heart chakra dynamics; contributes to conscious enlightenment state by activating attunement process through heart chakra function

ADAMITE: promotes astral travel and intensifies awareness of etheric body (see page 79)

ALUNITE: assists in balancing energies and evolved directives of heart chakra functions with lower chakra triad by stimulating integration, acceptance and application of principles of Divine Truth

AMAZONITE: harmonizes activities of heart and throat chakras, thereby assisting in establishing balanced emotional expressions (see page 83)

AMBER: ancient Earth vibration *(fossilized resin from cone bearing trees)* that assists mankind in comprehending dynamics of plant/animal interface; assists in drawing illness from physical body; aids in blood purification; strengthens and purifies physical and etheric body (see page 87)

AMETHYST QUARTZ: aids in calming the conscious mind by clearing third eye perceptions; aids in settling chaos and perceived contradictions of third dimension existence that impede ability to clearly see elements of evolutionary journey (see page 93)

AMETRINE: combination of Amethyst and Citrine Quartz promotes clear thought processes that enable the application of Etheric Wisdom to emerge in behavior patterns

ANHYDRITE: stimulates astral states and provides gentle transition between third dimension and the celestial realm

APATITE(Blue): opens and stabilizes energies of the throat chakra; helps reduce episodes of stuttering (see page 99)

APATITE (Yellow): assists in stabilizing will power dynamics of solar plexus; aids in building and/or regenerating muscle tissues

APOPHYLLITE: facilitates crown chakra and third eye acceptance of the etheric body's contact with and involvement in the conscious application of Divine Truth (see page 103)

AQUAMARINE: impacts upon endocrine system *(thymus gland)* to reduce nervous tension; aids in the evolution of the throat chakra to verbalize inner truths that reveal true dynamics of self

ARAGONITE: strengthens chakra cord to allow greater volume of Divine Light Vibration transmission, and in so doing, facilitates greater understanding of the nature and dynamics of one's higher self

ATACAMITE: aids in integrating Etheric Constructs of Peace and Tranquility with emotional expressions (see page 107)

AVENTURINE: physical and emotional balancer; channels crown chakra vibrations *(golden ray)* into the energy matrix of the body through the soothing, green vibration of Mother Earth (see page 111)

AZULICITE: meridian chakra balancer (see page 115)

AZURITE: purger of third eye congestion *(inner thought modes)*; often ruthless in surfacing innermost dynamics of thought process

BARITE: (Desert Rose) transmits Tranquil vibrations to facilitate harmonious interactions in situations of high-pitched mental and/or physical activity; impacts upon mental and emotional systems to generate cooperative attitudes in interpersonal and working relationships

BLOODSTONE: aids in cleansing and strengthening circulatory system; strengthens immune system, thereby impacting upon all physical modalities of well-being

BLUE LACE AGATE: reduces nervous tension and relieves tension headaches; assists in opening throat chakra to facilitate Peaceful verbal expressions; soothes upset or irritated physical and emotional systems with benevolent energy of the light blue ray

BOJI STONE: Iron ore compound *(crystallized)* that promotes electrical balance throughout physical body; aids in balancing hyperactivity

CALCITE: integrates Etheric Consciousness with mental processes to assist in the assimilation and expression of Universal Law and Divine Will (see page 117)

CARNELIAN: amplifies Earth energy at lower vibratory rate than other Quartz silicates; connects soul incarnate's consciousness with the dynamics of Mother Earth's evolution

CELESTITE: enhancer of astral states; encourages the expression of Etheric Wisdom through conscious thought modes (see page 123)

CHALCOPYRITE: enhancer of mental and/or visionary states; facilitates creativity and endurance; elevator of third eye and crown chakra vibrations

CHRYSOCOLLA: emotional balancer; facilitates hormonal balance (see page 127)

CHRYSOPRASE: aids in the development of altruistic expressions of Love; assists in transmuting self-serving, egocentric energies

CHRYSOTILE: assists in drawing toxic vibrations from heart, solar plexus and navel chakra areas

CITRINE QUARTZ: assists in channeling the golden ray of the crown chakra *(through which Etheric Wisdom flows)* into the navel chakra for the physical expression of Divine Truth upon the Earth Plane; aids in digestive functions (see page 131)

COVELLITE: actuates third eye vibrations as it eases emotional conflicts associated with heart chakra function

CUPRITE: facilitates opening and balancing of heart chakra energies

DANBERITE: opens crown chakra to receive elements of Higher Consciousness; energizes chakra system by transmitting higher volume of Divine Light Vibrations along chakra cord

DENDRITIC AGATE: illustrates the transition mode between plant and animal Kingdoms that conveys to mankind the proposition that different thoughts, feelings and conditions can be harmoniously interfaced

DIOPTASE: encourages one to take the time to "smell the roses" along life's highway by assisting one to release the confining, manipulative, conditioned behavior patterns that stress absolute devotion to duty in a materialistic society; assists in counter-balancing attitudes that lead one to take one's position or responsibility too seriously; stimulates playfulness (see page 135)

DRAVITE (Brown Tourmaline): facilitates transmutation of discordant emotional energies from solar plexus and navel chakra; restores vital energy and grounding vibration to will power dynamics (see page 231)

EILAT: combination of copper related minerals *(Chrysocolla, Turquoise, Azurite, Malachite)* that facilitate release of emotional energy and aid in balancing of energy systems associated with third eye, throat, heart and solar plexus chakras

ELBAITE (Green Tourmaline): stimulates Healing Facilitation of both nerve and organ systems of the body; stimulates immune system functions (see page 231)

ELESTIAL QUARTZ: assists mankind in penetrating the layers of consciousness to identify core motivations for discordant behavior patterns (see page 139)

EMERALD: transmits calming influence to mental processes; stimulates optimal functioning of all heart chakra dynamics; promotes emotional understanding, Mercy, altruistic consideration and Love

EPIDOTE: assists in integrating and focusing aspects of consciousness that have become stressed, separated or misaligned as a result of denial or emotional trauma, thereby increasing one's personal sense of Knowingness through enhanced clarity of perception; impacts energies of heart chakra, third eye *(both front and rear)* and crown chakra regions

FIRE AGATE: dynamic grounding vibration that combines elements of Earth and Fire; assists with determination and execution of tasks necessary for the evolution of Light-minded behavior (see page 143)

FLUORITE: assists in channeling dynamics of Etheric Order into the conscious mind through third eye function; assists in grounding the comprehension of Etheric Order into the conscious mind (see page 147)

GARNET: assists in lower navel and base chakra development of conscionable sense of determination

GOETHITE: stimulates general sense of inner Peace and Tranquility, as if one had been caressed and washed free of discordance by gentle, Compassionate ocean waves

GOLD: transmits solar, masculine energies to assist in stabilization and grounding of all systems

HEMATITE: focuses Earth vibration to assist as grounding agent; assists in the lessening and/or removal of physical pain by its placement upon the site of the injury

HERKIMER DIAMONDS: double terminated Clear Quartz Crystals endowed with an exceptionally high Divine Light Vibration that are found in Herkimer County, New York

INDICOLITE: (Blue Tourmaline) promotes energy balancing and transformation of emotional traumas associated with throat chakra (see page 231)

IOLITE: clears and opens crown, third eye and throat chakras; assists in the integration of Etheric Wisdom with the conscious thought process to enhance perception abilities, thereby enabling dynamic comprehension of Earthly/Etheric Truths

JADE: amplifies facilitating Earth vibrations that are utilized by heart chakra to stimulate physical well-being

KUNZITE: integrates third eye dynamics with heart chakra function, thereby giving birth to Compassion (see page 151)

KYANITE: aids in transmuting fears and anxieties associated with throat chakra (see page 155)

KYANITE WING (Black): assists in balancing and grounding Divine Light Vibrations throughout the physical body

LABRADORITE: heightens perceptions of spatial relationships; improves night vision

LAPIS LAZULI: aids in accessing deepest levels of inner truth, as well as highest levels of Etheric Truth; aids in reducing tension and stress that precipitate stiffness in the neck, shoulders and upper back (see page 159)

LARIMAR: calming, soothing vibration of sky and water; particularly beneficial for stimulating transformation of emotional wounds associated with the throat chakra

LAZULITE: opens, calms and stimulates clarity and well-being of third eye vibrations; transmits Tranquil energy throughout entire chakra system

LEOPARDSKIN AGATE: stimulates Peaceful, grounding sensations throughout the physical body

LEPIDOLITE/RUBELLITE: emotional calming agent *(Lithium content)*; Rubellite *(Pink Tourmaline)* within matrix serves to heighten well-being of heart chakra that transmits Peaceful, Loving vibration through entire system

MALACHITE: amplifies vibration that aids in identifying and surfacing emotional traumas attached to heart chakra and/or solar plexus (see page 163)

MARCASITE: facilitates the development of Etheric Consciousness; assists in the acceptance of Etheric Truth through solar plexus and navel chakra activity; facilitates the application of Etheric Consciousness through one's expression of personal reality

METEORITE: stimulates past life memory of other planetary systems, as well as perceptions of ongoing extraterrestrial activity in current incarnation (see page 169)

MOLDAVITE: facilitates third eye transformation; enhances ability to clearly perceive reality of truth; amplifies consciousness-raising vibrations associated with the star-group Pleiades

MOONSTONE: emotional balancer; aids in balancing emotional dysfunctions through crown, third eye and heart chakra integration and transmutation of discordant vibrations (see page 173)

MOSS AGATE: promotes improved circulatory and digestive functions

NEPTUNITE: stimulates base chakra vibrations to activate Kundalini energy

OBSIDIAN: deep grounding vibration; repels discordant energies (see page 177)

ONYX: intensifies reception of Etheric Vibrations; enhances visionary perceptions

OPAL: intensifies and accelerates emotional states

ORTHOCLASE: facilitates the unfoldment of heart chakra dynamics within the deepest states of Meditation (see page 183)

PAMPA ONYX: transmits facilitating, balancing energies into lower heart chakra and solar plexus to assist in uniform Divine Light transmission along chakra cord; stimulates visionary sequences and awakens memories of altered states of consciousness

PERIDOT: amplifies facilitating green ray that impacts upon heart chakra and organ systems associated with solar plexus and navel chakras; affects regeneration modes of the immune system (see page 187)

PETRIFIED WOOD: facilitates past life recall during Meditation;

promotes tissue regeneration and offers protection against infection

PICTURE JASPER: stabilizes and grounds physical energies of solar plexus, navel and base chakras; facilitates visualization processes by integrating functions of left and right brain activity in Meditation

PLUME AGATE: promotes facilitating vibrations in navel and base chakras

PREHNITE: amplifies Meditative and Astral experiences by stimulating intuitive understanding

PYRITE: facilitates crown chakra and third eye energies that assist in the attainment and maintenance of clarity in the conscious mind

PYROPHYLLITE: generates centered, calming effect through crown to navel chakras and assists in integration and grounding

REALGAR: stimulates navel and upper base chakra dynamics as related to increased efficiency in digestion and reproduction

RHODOCROSITE: functions as a bridging element for the upper and lower chakra triads by facilitating energy exchanges and transfers between heart chakra and solar plexus that serve to balance energy matrix (see page 195)

RHODONITE: facilitates the release of self-abasing tension and emotions to establish grounded sense of self-worth

RHYOLITE: volcanic formation that aids in balancing and/or integrating right and left brain functions, thereby unifying the expression of masculine and feminine vibrations

ROSE QUARTZ: amplifies the pink ray that facilitates transformation of emotional wounds associated with the heart chakra; aids in transforming emotional wounds of the entire energy matrix (see page 199)

RUBELLITE (Pink Tourmaline): generates Compassionate, nurturing vibration to any emotionally discordant system of the body, especially the heart and solar plexus chakras (see page 231)

RUBY: intensifies passion for life and ability to Love; stimulates courage and devotion; promotes heart chakra function and aids in circulation; energizes both physical and emotional systems

RUTILATED QUARTZ: golden rutiles (needles of basalt) within Quartz Crystal matrix; channels golden ray of the crown chakra into the navel chakra to assist in the implementation of Divine Will upon the Earth Plane

SAPPHIRE: promotes mental calm and stability through the establishment of intuition, order and self-discipline; aids assimilation on physical level by assisting blood flow to organs of the abdominal cavity

SATIN KYANITE: activates crown chakra and stimulates rear third eye opening; permits greater volume of Divine Light Vibrations to be transmitted along the chakra cord and assists in balancing electrical transmission between the seven primary chakras

SCHORL (Black Tourmaline): repels discordant, hostile and/or aggressive vibrations that impact upon survival (base chakra)

modes (see page 232)

SELENITE: activates crown chakra to open and accept elements of Higher Truth *(Clear Selenite Crystals)* (see page 203)

SILVER: transmits lunar, feminine energies to assist in emotional and mental balancing

SMITHSONITE: integrates emotional and etheric bodies to generate Compassionate understanding and release from dysfunctional behavior patterns (see page 207)

SMOKY QUARTZ: generates Etheric Vibrations of the crown chakra for expression through the base chakra; grounding energy transmission that integrates Etheric Wisdom with the survival modes of Earthly reality (see page 211)

SODALITE: aids in clearing third dimension thought forms that breed confusion, and in so doing assists in establishing third eye clarity; affects stabilization of thyroid; facilitates the expression of true nature of self; reduces inclinations for self-abasement and transmutes guilts, fears and anxieties

SPURRITE (Strombolite): generates calming, electrical balance to the energy systems of the body; facilitates grounding and perceptions free of emotional influence

STIBNITE: facilitates merging of etheric self with heart chakra function by providing access mode through crown chakra to allow entry of etheric self; grounds transition of etheric energy with base chakra activity to stimulate balanced expression of Divine Truth in third dimension; provides calming influence while integrating dynamics of etheric and physical bodies

STILBITE: facilitates the acceptance of the temporal condition of physical reality and assists in the release of mortal consciousness from the physical body to further engage the reincarnate journeys of Soul Evolution

SUGILITE: helps reduce emotional impact of harsh realities encountered in daily life; aids in balancing one's perception of Earthly existence; assists in processing and transmuting aggressive energies and/or emotional traumas associated with the third eye (see page 215)

SULFUR: assists in drawing toxins and impurities from the body and aids in strengthening immune system functions

SUNSTONE: assists in developing the "cooperation mode" of behavior by transforming the egocentric nature of personal will within solar plexus dynamics into behavior inspired by understanding the teachings of Divine Will

THULITE: stimulates the coordination and elevation of heart chakra states, dynamics and function through unification and implementation of evolved, Light-minded purpose and intent

TIGER EYE: aids in grounding Etheric Consciousness into navel chakra and upper base chakra to assist in integrating etheric, crown chakra vibrations with the dynamics of survival modes (see page 219)

TOPAZ: White and Golden Topaz amplify vibrations that open and activate the crown chakra to receive Divine Light Energy of Absolute Truth; Yellow, Orange and Red Topaz impact upon the solar plexus and navel chakras assisting the digestive processes and facilitating the expressions of Light-minded behavior

TOURMALATED QUARTZ: Black Tourmaline Crystals within Clear Quartz matrix serve to help repel and disperse discordant energy vibrations

TOURMALINE: see Indicolite, Rubellite, Elbaite, Dravite, Schorl and Watermelon (see page 231)

TURQUOISE: assists in the assimilation and transmission of Etheric Wisdom through the spoken word (see page 235)

ULEXITE: stimulates crown chakra to assist in balancing emotional energies; engages modes of nervous tension to assist in attaining and/or maintaining balance of neurological transmissions

UNAKITE: pink and green rays stimulate well-being of heart chakra states; stimulates acceptance of the intuitive voice by stimulating dynamics of heart chakra functions

VANADINITE: assists in strengthening decision-making process and in implementing difficult choices

VARISCITE: aids in surfacing the reality of truth, the submerged emotional memories associated with the heart chakra, to assist in facilitating the deepest, most complete experience of heart chakra evolution

WATERMELON TOURMALINE: transmits facilitating pink and green rays into heart chakra area to transmute emotional and physical traumas; strengthens heart chakra dynamics to enable self-Love, forgiveness and trust to develop; impacts upon heart chakra dynamics by balancing electrical impulses and transmissions sent to and received from other areas of chakra system (see page 232)

WAVELLITE: stimulates the production of red blood cells and can be used in the treatment of bone cancer; promotes discernment abilities

WULFENITE: promotes release of toxins from spleen and digestive organs (see page 239)

YOUNGITE: activates third eye *(both front and rear)* and throat chakras to enhance perception and man's ability to effectively verbalize how he perceives reality; seeks to balance activity of the thyroid and pituitary glands

ZEBRA STONE (Zebra Marble): generates balancing, grounding energy systems that produce calming, contented sensations throughout the body; visually represents a state of inner knowingness and the application of the understanding that The Light and the darkness exist as One, thus transcending the illusion of Maya *(duality)*

ZOISITE (Green) with Hornblend and Ruby: assists in transforming lower heart chakra states of sorrow, guilt and self-pity into dynamic awareness, acceptance and understanding of emotional conditions by grounding and reinforcing Divine Light Vibrations along entire chakra cord, while strengthening determination and drive toward God-Realized Truth

IV

Crystal & Mineral Combinations

Many combinations of Crystals and Minerals are used in facilitation sessions at Portal Enterprises to assist clients in uncovering and transmuting discordant energy systems. The list that follows details some of the most frequently used Mineral combinations. Each combination is described in terms of the application and the particular results that can be experienced. However, it is recommended that the information given below be used as the foundation upon which you allow your intuition and experience to build your knowledge of the properties and the results that can be effected by Crystal and Mineral combinations. *(For self-application of Mineral combinations, first initiate a deep-breathing sequence to induce relaxation. Then while holding Crystals or after placing them upon your body, silently repeat the words, "Attune, Balance, Integrate, Ground." Relax and allow your energy matrix to absorb The Divine Light Vibrations amplified through your Crystals.)*

ADAMITE/ULEXITE: initiates astral states and/or visionary sequences of high Divine Light Vibration when both Crystals are held together in left hand

AMETHYST/MOONSTONE: soothes conscious mind and calms emotions to enable clear thought processes to take place; Crystals can be placed together directly upon third eye center for periods up to ten minutes per application

APATITE/BLUE LACE AGATE: (Blue Apatite) promotes calm energy transmission through the throat chakra and reduces emotional stress that results in inability to articulate feelings; hold both Crystals at throat chakra with left hand

APOPHYLLITE/LAPIS LAZULI: facilitates crown chakra and third eye acceptance of the etheric body's contact with and involvement in the conscious application of Divine Truth, while

319

simultaneously aiding in the release of accumulated tensions and stress related to feelings of self-doubt and unworthiness; facilitates the awakening to those aspects of consciousness that are Universally "good and right" for the evolution of all things born of Creation; hold Apophyllite against front third eye with the right hand and hold Lapis against rear third eye with the left hand *(Lapis can be moved from ear to ear along the back of the neck and returned to rear third eye)*

ATACAMITE/LAPIS LAZULI/ROSE QUARTZ: balances and facilitates emotional energy to allow for elements of inner truth to surface and become integrated into personal reality; place Atacamite and Lapis upon third eye center with right hand, while holding Rose Quartz at rear third eye with left hand

AZURITE/MALACHITE/ROSE QUARTZ: Azurite/Malachite combination when placed upon third eye, throat or heart chakra will surface emotional traumas that cause energy blockages and/or imbalances; Rose Quartz is then applied to the site to facilitate the transformation of opened emotional wounds

BOJI STONE/KYANITE WING: aligns and balances energy systems, while simultaneously repairing lacerations in auric energy matrix; hold Boji Stone in right hand and Kyanite Wing in left hand

CHRYSOPRASE/LAPIS LAZULI: facilitates acknowledgement and release of counterproductive aspects of one's inner emotional being; hold Lapis against third eye with left hand and Chrysoprase against heart chakra with right hand

CITRINE/HONEY CALCITE/CARNELIAN: integrates etheric designs of Universal Law with Earth energy dynamics - moving from crown to navel chakra; hold Crystals in place directly upon navel chakra

CLEAR OPTICAL CALCITE RHOMBOID (Iceland Spar)/ SNOWFLAKE OBSIDIAN/ROSE QUARTZ: to discharge excess energies about crown and third eye chakras that cause tension and migraine headaches, hold Calcite and Obsidian against third eye center with right hand and hold Rose Quartz against rear third eye with left hand for three to five minutes

EILAT/CHRYSOCOLLA/MOONSTONE: soothes overwrought emotional conditions and aligns emotional energies so that clear understanding and expression of one's reality can take place; Crystals may be held together in left hand to initiate attunement

EMERALD/ELBAITE/RUBY: facilitates optimal functioning of physical, mental and emotional systems; place each Crystal upon heart chakra and hold in place with left hand, then place right hand over left hand

FIRE AGATE/GARNET/SMOKY QUARTZ: transmits grounding and determination at base and navel chakra levels to facilitate Light-minded execution of survival drives; hold Crystals together in left hand for attunement or place directly upon lower navel and base chakras to absorb vibrations

FLUORITE/PYRITE: helps to integrate constructs of etheric organization into the dynamics of the conscious thought process when held in place at the crown and third eye chakras; hold Fluorite with the left hand against the crown chakra and hold the Pyrite with the right hand at the third eye center

GOLD SHEEN OBSIDIAN/SMOKY QUARTZ: dramatically channels the Golden/White Light Vibrations of Divine Truth into the base chakra for the purpose of grounding The into the base chakra for the purpose of grounding The Consciousness of One into the daily decision-making process; both Crystals can be held together in the left hand

GREEN CALCITE/LAPIS LAZULI: provides clarity of inner truth and aids in soothing an overworked conscious mind; both Minerals can be held in the left hand for attunement, or Green Calcite can be placed on the third eye with right hand and Lapis held on the rear third eye with left hand

HEMATITE/SHEEN OBSIDIAN: hold both in left hand to heighten sense of grounding through the base chakra and to provide a sense of connection to and recognition of Earthly reality

INDICOLITE/RUBELLITE/TURQUOISE: Indicolite/Rubellite, a Blue Tourmaline Crystal that terminates in Pink/Red Tourmaline can be applied to the throat chakra with the right hand for 2-3 minutes to open throat chakra and transmute blockages; Turquoise can then be applied to site with the right hand to facilitate flow of Etheric Wisdom in speech pattern

KUNZITE/SUGILITE: helps to generate sense of Compassion in one's perceptions of discordant energy sources; either hold both Crystals in left hand for attunement, or place Sugilite upon third eye and Kunzite upon the heart chakra

LAPIS LAZULI/ROSE QUARTZ: helps to release one from self-recriminating judgments and stimulates transformation of discordant emotional vibrations; place Lapis at rear third eye, then rub it along the neck from ear to ear with the right hand, while Rose Quartz is held with the left hand at third eye center

MALACHITE/ROSE QUARTZ/RHODOCHROSITE: helps to surface and transmute discordant energy systems attached to the heart and solar plexus chakras, then facilitates the integration and balance of energy exchange between the upper and lower chakra triads; Crystals can be held in the left hand or placed directly upon the heart center and solar plexus chakra

RAINBOW OBSIDIAN/SUGILITE: helps ground conscious acceptance of third dimension realities without becoming adversely affected by harsh behaviors exhibited by others; protects sensitive, gentle soul incarnates from discordant, belligerent vibrations; Minerals may be held in left hand for attunement or Sugilite can be placed on third eye with left hand and Rainbow Obsidian held against base chakra with right hand

RHODOCHROSITE/LEPIDOLITE/RUBELLITE: generates calming, balancing energy transmissions along entire chakra cord; Crystals may be held in the left hand or placed directly upon the heart chakra

RHYOLITE/CHRYSOCOLLA: aids in the balancing of masculine/feminine energies, while rectifying hormonal imbalances; balances emotional energies; attune by holding Minerals in left hand or by placing Minerals upon heart, solar plexus and navel chakras

ROSE QUARTZ/LEPIDOLITE/RUBELLITE: place upon heart chakra to assist in comforting and quieting frazzled nerves and/or emotional wounds resultant from discordant interpersonal relationships

RUTILATED QUARTZ/MAHOGANY OBSIDIAN: transmits dynamics of Universal Law into the "work ethic" of navel and base chakras; enables one to generate that which is "good and right" in cooperative endeavors; hold Crystals together in left hand

SHEEN OBSIDIAN/APOPHYLLITE: stimulates the release of discordant energy systems from rear third eye, while grounding elements of Divine Truth into consciousness and infusing third eye center with Divine Light Vibrations that expand level of consciousness and facilitate clarity of perception; rub Obsidian (*egg or sphere*) against back of neck from ear to ear and then hold it in place against rear third eye with the left hand; hold Apophyllite against front third eye with the right hand

SMITHSONITE/CHRYSOCOLLA/AMETHYST: promotes integration and balance of emotional, mental and etheric bodies, while facilitating conscious understanding of emotional constructs; Minerals may be held together in the left hand for attunement, or Smithsonite and Amethyst can be held on third eye with left hand and Chrysocolla held on the navel chakra with the right hand

SPURRITE/KYANITE: Green and Blue Kyanite Crystals when held with Spurrite in the left hand produce a sense of alignment and integration of the etheric, physical and emotional bodies

SULPHUR/WULFENITE/AMBER: aids in drawing toxins from abdominal cavity, while strengthening solar plexus and navel chakra energies; place Minerals and Amber directly upon abdominal cavity from solar plexus to navel chakra

VARISCITE/PERIDOT/AVENTURINE/ELBAITE: when these Crystals are placed upon the heart center and are attuned to, they initiate and provide a penetrating, transformational vibration that impacts upon the entire physical system; to a slightly lesser degree   these Minerals initiate facilitation upon the emotional level

WULFENITE/CHRYSOCOLLA: aids in purging toxins from spleen and digestive system, while balancing hormonal energies; aids in relieving symptoms associated with menstruation and/or menopause; hold Chrysocolla directly upon navel with right hand and hold Wulfenite at navel chakra with left hand

V

*Glossary and Guide to
Spiritual/Metaphysical Terms*

ABSOLUTE TRUTH: principles of Universal Law and Divine Will that hold true in application throughout the realm of existence

ADONAI: The Lord God *(Hebrew)*

AFFIRMATION: the declaration and the process of instilling Light-minded thoughts and behavior patterns within the conscious mind

AKASHA: in Hindu Tradition, the etheric, elemental material from which all physical reality is created

ALCHEMY: the science and practice of transmutation and transformation, especially as pertains to the infusion of greater volumes of Divine Light Vibrations into matter and consciousness

ALLAH: in Islamic tradition, the Supreme, Universal Being through Whom all Creation was conceived

ARCHANGEL: the energy presence of a specific element of The God Spirit invoked to facilitate and/or to provide guidance in the execution of a specific Earthly task; the purest, most dynamic, most evolved vibrations within the Angelic Order

AROMATHERAPY: the use of fragrances to stimulate conditions of physical, mental, emotional and spiritual well-being; contemporary therapeutic uses of fragrances are based upon Ayurvedic Tradition

ASCENDED TEACHER: disembodied Initiate of The Light of One who has learned the application of Universal Law within third dimension framework, and who offers The Wisdom of One to evolving soul incarnates through channel and visionary sequences

ASCETIC: an aspirant or earnest seeker who leads a life of Selflessness and self-discipline in keeping with religious/spiritual doctrines to achieve an enlightened state of consciousness through practices of Meditation and self-denial

ASTRAL PROJECTION: the process of propelling one's consciousness beyond third dimension reality to glean galactic truths relevant to Earthly existence

AURA/AURIC BODY: pattern of Divine Light Vibrations broken down into individual color spectrums or bands that surround and penetrate the physical body

AURIC SYSTEM: states or energy planes of conscious existence

AVATAR: the descent of The Divine Spirit into the flesh of mortal man; the incarnate form of The Living God Spirit in the body of man *(Hindu)*

BRAHMA: in Hindu Theology, the Absolute, Eternal Essence of the Universe; the Source of all things

BUDDHISM: religious and philosophic tradition of central and eastern Asia founded in India in the 6th Century B.C. by Gautama Siddhartha *(Buddha)* that teaches that "right living", "right thinking" and self-denial will enable the soul to reach the Divine state of release from Earthly and bodily pain, sorrow and desire known as Nirvana

CAUSAL BODY: aspect of conscious being in which mental impressions are formed

CHAKRA CORD: energy system that surrounds and permeates spinal column and connects crown chakra to base chakra with Divine Light Vibrations transmissions

CHAKRA(S): energy centers about the physical body that regulate the flow of Divine Light Vibrations throughout the body, and the evolution of which impacts upon one's ability to assimilate elements of Higher Consciousness

CHANNELING: the act of accessing intuitive and/or etheric information for problem solving or guidance in negotiating mortal life

CHI: in Chinese philosophy, the energy system of the "life-force"

CLAIRAUDIENCE: the ability to perceive sounds thought usually to be inaudible in the physical plane, as in perceiving channeled transmissions from etheric sources

CLAIRVOYANCE: the ability to perceive objects, thoughts and/or behavior patterns not present or apparent to the five basic senses

CONDUIT: soul initiate who shares continuous conscious mind-link with etheric being or social memory complex

COUNCIL OF TWELVE, THE: The Etheric Unit responsible for the galactic plan of Earth; The Oversouls; the unit of twelve, evolved social memory complexes that define, represent and promulgate The Conscience and Wisdom of One

COSMIC ILLUMINATION: instances of etheric transmissions that may last a few minutes, hours or days during which a soul initiate, seemingly suspended in time and space, receives information regarding Divine Order and Operation *(the nature, dynamics and function of Creation)*

DEVA/DEVIC PRESENCE: elemental vibrations *(life forms)* that exist and work within the water, upon and within the land and in the air to assist in affecting and maintaining balance within and between the various Kingdoms of Mother Earth

DHARMA: the path of righteousness or simply "right-living" as defined by the customs and rules of society *(Hindu)*

DIVINATION: an act or attempt to foretell future events or the nature of probable life-conditions

DIVINE WILL: Universal Order that impacts upon and guides the course of Creation toward The Resolution of One

DORJE: Tibetan tool of balance and Compassion; energy wand composed of two single terminated Clear Quartz Crystals of equal size and strength set into wand shaft with apexes pointed in opposite directions away from center of shaft

DOUBLE TERMINATED CRYSTAL: Crystal that has formed termination apexes at both ends of the Crystal shaft; may be natural formation or a man-made, polished Crystal

EGO-SELF: the temporal state of mortal consciousness that seeks to actualize conditions of pleasure, survival, control, possession, dominance, manipulation and self-importance; the energy matrix through which all compelling emotions and desires are expressed

ENERGY MATRIX: system of Divine Light Vibrations that form patterns of consciousness on physical, mental and spiritual planes

ENLIGHTENMENT: the ongoing, unfoldment process by which mortal man assimilates The Wisdom of One

ETHERIC SYSTEM: elements of everlasting Spiritual Truth accessed through evolved consciousness states

EVOCATION: a calling forth or summoning of disembodied spirit presence to perform tasks of self-serving interests

FETISH: tool, carving, icon or doll endowed with spiritual powers designed to protect, grant fertility or abundant crops, guide in decision-making, strengthen in battle or repel hostile energies from its owner

FOURTH DIMENSION: the vibratory rate denoting "Christ Consciousness", Etheric Love and heart-centered behavior; the next quantum octave of conscious existence from that of the Earth Plane or third dimension, physical reality

GENERATOR POINT: single terminated Quartz Crystal (*usually Clear Quartz, but Smoky, Amethyst and Citrine Quartz Points can also be used as Generators*) used to amplify and direct Divine Light Vibrations for Healing Facilitation and/or Meditation

GOD-REALIZED CONSCIOUSNESS: thoughts, behaviors and energies motivated by Selflessness; the Patience, Compassion, Wisdom, Mercy, Serenity and Love to willingly and unilaterally apply Universal Law upon the Earth Plane; state of conscious being that allows all perceptions to be generated through the open, evolved heart chakra center

GOD-SELF: the evolved energy matrix of an open heart chakra through which Intuitive Wisdom guides mortal man in the implementation of Light-minded behavior

GROSS BODY: aspect of consciousness through which physical reality is perceived

HARVEST: the period of time at the end of each Karmic Cycle *(approximately every 65,000 years)* when the evolved soul vibrations of mortal man are etherically prepared to pass from 3rd density Earth consciousness to 4th density Christ-Consciousness

HEALING FACILITATION: the act of assisting another mortal being in the release and transmutation of discordant energy systems from mortal consciousness by the application and infusion of Divine Light Vibrations

HOMEOSTASIS: the dynamic state of balance or equilibrium that is sought by the elements of a system

INTUITIVE VOICE: the subconscious motivations of God-Realization that guide each mortal incarnate toward the achievement of his/her most actualized spiritual state within third dimension

INVOCATION: the process of calling upon Divine Presence and/or Divine Light Vibrations to assist in spiritual activity

JAH: abbreviation for the name of The God Spirit Jehovah

KABBALAH: ancient Hebrew mystical system of divination; system that explains the consciousness of the Universe and man's place within Divine Order

KARMA: the law of retribution or the law of cause and effect, action and reaction, as applied to the reincarnate life cycles of mortal beings *(Hindu)*

KARMIC RESOLUTION: the process of identifying and breaking the bonds of conditioning that perpetuate discordant, counter-productive behavior patterns

KETHER: in Kabbalistic tradition, the ultimate, Creative Source within the Universe that is beyond the comprehension of mortal man

KINDRED SPIRIT: soul incarnate who vibrates with similar patterns of knowledge and life-experience, and with whom concurrent and/or similar reincarnate journeys can be identified

KUNDALINI: primal energy force that when awakened allows mortal man to experience his/her cosmic connection to all things born of Creation; swirling energy force that rises from base chakra opening and penetrating each chakra enroute to and including the crown chakra that affords mortal consciousness a connection mode with elements of Divine Truth

LIGHT-MINDED BEHAVIOR: behaviors designed to attain and maintain enlightened states of consciousness and focused upon man's ability to service all things born of Creation

LINEAR THOUGHT: the logical, analytical, left-brain thought process that employs deduction, rationalization and empirical reasoning to explain the conditions and experience of Universal Existence

MANIFESTATION: an act or attempt to create reality that ultimately interferes with the natural order of existence

MANTRAS: sacred sound syllables and/or words used in Hindu worship that invoke changes in energy, consciousness and being; also used in Buddhism and other traditions that employ "ritual chanting"

MAYA: in Hindu philosophy, the "cosmic illusion" of duality which mortal man has been charged to transcend in order to discover The Divine God Spirit alive in The Oneness of Creation

MEDITATION: clearing the conscious mind of the active thought process to allow and foster communion with the internal Peace and guidance of the Intuitive Wisdom of the soul

OM (Aum): the cosmic creative vibration; the "sound" of the The Universal God *(Hindu)*

ORION: confederation of etheric beings who oppose the presence, dynamics and function of The Council of Twelve; responsible for channeling great volumes of information to mortal consciousness that are ultimately designed to aggrandize self; responsible for extraterrestrial visitations, crop circles, abductions and interventions upon evolutionary process of The Earth Colony

PHENOMENAL SYSTEM: the continuum of physical existence

PLEIADES: star group within the constellation Taurus

PRANA: in Hindu philosophy, the "life-force" that is the energy system that pervades the Universe and is responsible for Creation

PSYCHOMETRY: the process of divining knowledge about an object or a person connected with that object through contact with the object

REAR THIRD EYE: area at the back of the head just above the point at which the skull and neck unite; area covered by occipital bone

RESONANCE: the vibrational frequency or "pitch" at which or through which transmission and reception of thought pattern energy states are acknowledged, effected or produced

SHAMAN: one of tribal and Earth Consciousness indoctrination and initiation, who through invocation of and communion with spirit beings gleans insights and problem solving information to assist tribal group

SHAMBHALA: system of Tibetan teachings founded upon Buddhism that reflects traditions of "warriorship" - human bravery, Selflessness, Compassion, Wisdom and Mercy; tradition acknowledges that an inherent state of wakefulness, sanity, Wisdom and Compassion exist as potential within every mortal being that can be tapped to solve the problematic conditions faced by society; the sacred path of the Peaceful Warrior

SHIVA LINGAM: stone phallus used in the worship of the Hindu God Shiva; Tantric Meditation Tool used to activate "life-force" energies and to assist in connecting mortal consciousness to the creative flow of the Universe

SIRIUS: the star group from which all galactic life was spawned; located in the constellation Canis Major; the brightest star in the heavens; birthplace of The Yahweh Entity

SOCIAL MEMORY COMPLEX: the evolved, collective consciousness of a civilization that no longer exists in physical form, but whose collective energy and incarnate memory exist as one dynamic, homogeneous system of knowledge

SOUL: the essence of life-consciousness; memory matrix that records behavior patterns, emotions and life-experiences of evolving incarnate being

SOUL ESSENCE: the energy matrix that defines the memory pattern of consciousness

SOUL EVOLUTION: the reincarnate journeys of time that allow each soul incarnate the opportunity to assimilate The Lessons of Existence, thereby comprehending and applying The Wisdom of One

SOUL INCARNATE: the physical embodiment of man as he endeavors to find his place and function within galactic order

SOUL INITIATE: an evolved soul incarnate who understands and applies The Absolute Wisdom of One

SOUL MATE: soul incarnate *(sexual counterpart)* who exhibits complementary and supplementary behaviors, knowledge and life-experience to enable a free, naturally harmonious Love-filled relationship to evolve; soul incarnate who may have been Loving mate in past reincarnations

SPIRIT GUIDE: disembodied soul consciousness that offers clues and/or assistance in negotiating mortal existence

SPIRITUAL ATTUNEMENT: the process of accessing the source of Divine Light Vibration within human consciousness that is the "soul-link" to The Infinite Body of God

SPIRITUALISM: a way of life that acknowledges and applauds all things born of Creation as being sacred; the consciousness that all things born of Creation contain the same LoveLight Vibration, and proclaims that the varied Kingdoms of Mother Earth are brethren

SUBTLE BODY: aspect of conscious being through which energies of "life-force" are perceived

SYNERGY: the combined or cooperative action or force that makes the resultant activity greater than the sum of its parts

THE INFINITE ONE: The Absolute Source of all Galactic Creation

TRANSCENDENCE: the process and state of consciousness that facilitates evolved perceptions of reality, which allows mortal consciousness to release and/or extinguish conditioned, reactionary, counterproductive behaviors, thereby allowing God-Realized perceptions to explain and to accept The Oneness of all things

TRANSDUCTION: the conversion of one form of energy into another

TRANSFORMATION: the active process of birthing and rebirthing that allows mankind to understand the dynamics and purpose of energy and behavioral changes as they take place, thereby facilitating the conscious transition from counter-productive, discordant behaviors to behaviors that illustrate an understanding of the true applications of Universal Law

TRANSMIGRATION: the act or process of passing from one physical consciousness state to another; the evolutionary process that allows the soul essence to pass from one vehicle of consciousness to another, as in the evolution of mortal consciousness through the other Kingdoms and lesser evolved physical forms of Earth

TRANSMUTATION: the process by which discordant energy is released from mortal consciousness, blessed and etherically balanced with harmonious energy vibrations

UNIVERSAL LAW: the body of Higher Truth that details the treatment and function of all life forms throughout the Universe

VORTEX: geomagnetic and/or electrical energy centers where heightened states of etheric communication and programming can occur

WAKAN TANKA: Native American name for The Supreme God Being, Creator of all things, as used by the tribes of the Lakota Nation

WISDOM OF ONE, THE: The Universal Acknowledgement that all things born of Creation contain the same Light-Life Energy of Consciousness and warrant conditions that foster Harmony, Love and Peace

YAH: abbreviation for the name of The God Spirit Yahweh, The Entity known as The Creator of modern man

YIN/YANG: in Chinese philosophy, the balance of opposing forces found throughout nature; the balance of masculine and feminine energies, which is essential in the evolution of an enlightened soul incarnate; balance of logical and creative energies

EPILOGUE

The contents of this text required several years to evolve into the present form. As the result of Meditation, Prayer and the hands-on application of Crystalline Properties in facilitating the well-being of human energy systems, we have developed the techniques described in this text. Though the research and application of Crystal/Mineral properties to human energy systems can be quite subjective, there are nevertheless many similarities between the Crystal/Mineral Properties we reported and the properties that appear in other texts. It is indeed encouraging to know that many who investigate The Divine Light transmission capabilities of the Quartz/Mineral Kingdom are reaching similar conclusions.

Conversely, because there are many different levels of consciousness through which information can be accessed to implement Divine Light Vibrations, there will be discussions and descriptions of Crystalline Properties that appear in this text and not in other texts. This should not be reason to stimulate speculation as to which source of information is more accurate or valid; rather, this should be reason for the seeker of enlightenment to follow his/her own intuitive voice in accepting or rejecting any aspect of the information contained in this or any other text. It is for each soul incarnate being to learn to utilize information in the most efficient, conscionable manner possible, acknowledging all spiritually inspired information as being purposeful, and choosing that which is good and right to be incorporated into one's present reality. Of course, there will be different moments of readiness for each individual to accept various constructs of Spiritual Truth, which means that valid information unsuitable for application today may be useful at a later date, during another level of consciousness or moment of personal need.

It is our hope at Portal Enterprises that those soul incarnate beings who are directed to read this text will find information in these pages that will inspire the awakening of Intuitive Wisdom, Truth and Love. And it is also our hope that in some small way the contents of this text may serve to accelerate mankind's conscious evolution in accessing and accepting The Light and The Wisdom of The Universal One.

Shalom

APPENDIX I
Index of Color Plates

APPENDIX II
Index of Charts, Diagrams, Figures & Illustrations

In acknowledgement of
The One Infinite Creator,
Who lives in all things
born of Creation -

Sri Akhenaton

PROOF READING
Paula Chenier
Marilyn Egbert
Janice Ellis
Marlene Iris
Gail Marten

STRAIGHT SHOTS
Cover and Text Photography

FLASHPRINT
Printing - Color Insert

CHECKMATE PREPRESS
Separations - Color Insert

THOMSON-SHORE, Inc.
Printing - Text and Cover

MARTEN GRAPHICS
Graphic Design
Typesetting
Illustrations
Cover Design

In acknowledgement of Judy Herrmann and Michael Starke of Straight Shots, two blessed souls of vision and conscience, whose photographic talents have expanded the dimension and elevated the quality of this text -

For their meticulous attention to presentation and detail, for their willingness to accommodate our needs and for the love, enthusiasm and wonderment they brought to this project -

We deeply appreciate and thank you both, Judy and Michael.

Be Ye Kept In Love And In Peace, Gentle Ones,
Be Ye Kept In Love And Peace.

Shalom

Sri Akhenaton

Photography by
Judy Herrmann *&* **Michael Starke**
STRAIGHT SHOTS
9017 Mendenhall Court, Suite E
Columbia, Maryland 21045
(410) 290-3910

COVER CREDITS

Our Fully Terminated, Clear Selenite Cluster
71/2" high x 61/2" wide x 51/2" deep

Purchased from Mr. Paulo C. Freire
ASSEX TRADING, INC.

Cover Concept
SRI AKHENATON

Cover Design
GAIL MARTEN

Cover Photograph
MICHAEL STARKE

In acknowledgement of our dearest supporters,
our associates and suppliers, for their dedication, cooperation,
encouragement, donations of time, energy and resources
and for the commitment of self through acts of Loving Kindness,
we extend our deepest appreciation to Eloise, Paula, Marilyn,
Janice, Marlene, Gail, Frank and Michael and Barbara.

With Blessings of Love and Peace,

Shalom

*In acknowledgement of your effort and consideration
in faithfully standing by us to help bring this text
to completion, we thank you, Gail -
God Bless, Shalom.*

SPECIAL NOTES

The author and publisher welcome comments regarding the nature and content of this text. Sri Akhenaton will personally answer letters received by the publisher.

Please address comments to:
Sri Akhenaton
c/o THE PORTAL PRESS
P. O. Box 1449, Columbia, Maryland 21044

Additional copies of this text can be obtained from the publisher by sending $21.95 plus $3.85 each for postage and handling *(Maryland residents please include 5% sales tax)* to the address above.

BOOKS BY SRI AKHENATON

DISCUSSIONS OF SPIRITUAL ATTUNEMENT AND SOUL
EVOLUTION, VOLUME II
$12.95 plus $3.85 postage and handling
(ISBN 0-9621839-5-4)

REFLECTIONS FROM THE GOLDEN MIND
$12.95 plus $3.85 postage and handling
(ISBN 0-9621839-6-2)

CRYSTAL COMMUNION: LOVELIGHT MEDITATIONS
$21.95 plus $3.85 postage and handling
(ISBN 0-9621839-4-6)

LOVING TOUCH: THE SACRED COVENANT
OF DIVINE COMMUNION
$21.95 plus $3.85 postage and handling
(ISBN 0-9621839-8-9)

THE DAWNING: COMING OF AGE
$11.95 plus $3.85 postage and handling
(ISBN 0-9621839-7-0)

PORTAL ENTERPRISES

Founded and administered by Sri Akhenaton, Portal Enterprises is a non-sectarian Spiritual Development Center designed to awaken the potential for God-Realized Consciousness in the hearts and deeds of mankind. Through continuing courses in LoveLight Meditation, Loving Touch Workshops and Intensives, weekly Spiritual Gatherings, Books and Spiritual Products specially prepared by Sri Akhenaton, Portal Enterprises offers earnest seekers of enlightenment conscionable tools with which to engage the ever unfolding path that leads to the assimilation of The Wisdom of One - The Universal Revelation that all things born of Creation contain the same Light/Life Presence of The Living God Spirit, and therefore warrant respect, Loving Kindness and conditions that foster Peace and Harmony.

At Portal, we embrace the reincarnate journeys of life with The Etheric Precepts of Patience, Compassion, Wisdom, Mercy, Serenity and Love filling the heart to affect The Greater Good of all things, without encroaching upon Choice of Free Will or manipulating, coercing or dictating single-minded philosophies and promulgating egocentric doctrines thought to outline the "austere, righteous path" that leads to Spiritual Fulfillment. Rather, through the application of Divine Conscience, each soul incarnate is assisted in uncovering his/her own God-evolved being, thereby facilitating each person's readiness and ability to become conscionable participants in and willing servants to the evolutionary process and needs of Creation. It is our practice and fervent hope that the evolving consciousness of mortal man continues to be embraced with compassionate understanding both now and in the days ahead, and that the services and products offered by Portal Enterprises will, in some small way, prove helpful in stimulating, affirming and assisting mankind's conscious ascension into The Infinite Body of God.

THE
PORTAL ENTERPRISES
Mail Order Catalog
of Consecrated Spiritual Products

Portal Enterprises offers a unique collection of Consecrated Spiritual Products that have been cleansed, blessed and prepared by Sri Akhenaton. Through Sri Akhenaton, Oils, Incenses and Crystals are charged with Divine Light Vibrations to enhance the resonance pattern of each item. This additional preparation ensures that the Consecrated Spiritual Products prepared at Portal Enterprises will resonate with optimum efficiency and the highest intensity within the spectrum of Divine Light.

For a copy of The Portal Enterprises Mail Order Catalog of Consecrated Spiritual Products *(Oils, Incenses, Crystals, Books)*, simply send request to:

PORTAL ENTERPRISES
P. O. Box 1449
Columbia, Maryland 21044
or
call us at (301) 317-5873

When in the Baltimore/Washington, D. C. metropolitan area, plan a visit to The Crystal Gallery at Portal Enterprises, where over 100 different varieties of Crystals & Minerals, Oils, Incenses and Spiritual Tools are displayed and offered for sale. Call or write in advance for Gallery hours and directions.

Photograph by Rich Riggins

AUTHOR PROFILE

An evolved Mystic and an innovative Teacher of diverse Esoteric, Spiritual Philosophies, Sri Akhenaton serves the needs of Creation by offering inspired, heart-centered principles of Divine Love and the profound simplicity of The Wisdom of One to seekers of enlightenment to help comfort and explain the experience of mortal life. Through Spiritual, intuitive and practical guidance that ultimately leads aspirants to the unfoldment of God-Conscious Being, Sri Akhenaton touches the hearts and fills the souls of those he embraces with The Light of The Living God Spirit to assist each person in comprehending the nature of the Spiritual Path, the purpose of life on Earth and in rediscovering the true meaning of being "a child of God".

Sri Akhenaton is a beacon of Truth and Love illuminating the darkness of uncertainty, fear, anger, suffering and disbelief with The Divine Radiance of The Light and Conscience of One, thereby revealing The Universal Acknowledgement that all things born of Creation contain the same Light/Life Vibration of Divine Consciousness, and warrant the same care, consideration and Loving Kindness that man would deem appropriate for him/herself.

It is with the deepest Sincerity and Conviction that Sri Akhenaton offers his life and consciousness as tools to transmit The Divine Light Energy of The One Infinite Creator, and in so doing, assist in facilitating the evolutionary moment of awakening to God-Conscious Being for the collective soul of man. Through his teachings and practice of "Trans-Cultural" Spiritual Consciousness, Sri Akhenaton embraces the journey of life with Serenity, Patience, Compassion and joyful wonderment, taking "one day, one step at a time", in his giving of Self for The Greater Good of all Creation.

Printed with Soy Ink
on Recycled Paper